T0311681

Innovation Leadership

A leader's ability to discover and implement innovations is crucial to adapting to changing technologies and customer preferences, enhancing employee creativity, developing new products, supporting market competitiveness, and sustaining economic growth. Gliddon and Rothwell provide an exciting and comprehensive resource for readers that are currently seeking to build success in organizations with new ideas. Innovation leadership involves synthesizing different leadership styles in organizations to influence employees to produce creative ideas, products, services, and solutions. It is a practice and an approach to organization development and organizational change. Innovation leadership commonly includes four basic stages, which are: (a) support for idea generation, (b) identifying innovations, (c) evaluating innovations, and (d) implementation. There are two types of innovations, including: (a) exploratory innovation, which involves generating brand new ideas, and (b) value-added innovation, which involves modifying and renewing ideas that already exist. The two fundamental leadership theories that are generally necessary for innovation leadership are path-goal theory and Leader Member Exchange theory.

The key role in the practice of innovation leadership is that of the innovation leader. However, there are currently multiple perspectives on the definition of an innovation leader. An individual in an organization, a group within an organization, the organization itself, and even a community, state, or nation can be considered an innovation leader. The book explores each of these perspectives on the definition of an innovation leader.

David G. Gliddon is Lead Faculty in the College of Business and Management at Colorado Technical University, USA. He earned his doctorate and undergraduate degrees from Pennsylvania State University, USA, and his Master's degree from the University of Scranton, USA. As part of his post-doctoral work, he earned certificates from MIT, Yale, and the University of Cambridge, UK. As a member of the White House Community Leaders program, Dr. Gliddon attended a White House briefing and met President Barack Obama and First Lady Michelle Obama at a White House reception.

William J. Rothwell, Ph.D., SPHR, SHRM-SCP, CPLP Fellow is President of Rothwell & Associates, Inc. and Rothwell & Associates, LLC. He is also a Professor-in-Charge of the Workforce Education and Development program, Department of Learning and Performance Systems, at Pennsylvania State University, University Park campus. He has authored, co-authored, edited, or co-edited 300 books, book chapters, and articles – including over 90 books. He has also worked as a consultant for over 40 multinational corporations, including Motorola China, General Motors, Ford, and many others.

Innovation Leadership

Edited by
David G. Gliddon and William J. Rothwell

LONDON AND NEW YORK

First published 2018 by Routledge

2 Park Square, Milton Park, Abingdon, Oxfordshire OX14 4RN

52 Vanderbilt Avenue, New York, NY 10017

Routledge is an imprint of the Taylor & Francis Group, an informa business

First issued in paperback 2020

British Library Cataloguing in Publication Data
A catalogue record for this book is available from the British Library

Library of Congress Cataloging in Publication Data
Names: Gliddon, David G., 1977- editor. | Rothwell, William J., 1951- editor.
Title: Innovation leadership / [edited by] David G. Gliddon and William J. Rothwell.
Description: 1 Edition. | New York : Routledge, 2018. | Includes index.
Identifiers: LCCN 2018002832 | ISBN 9781138036871 (hardback)
Subjects: LCSH: Creative ability in business. | Organizational change. | Management--Technological innovations.
Classification: LCC HD53 .I5643 2018 | DDC 658.4/06--dc23
LC record available at https://lccn.loc.gov/2018002832

ISBN: 978-1-138-03687-1 (hbk)
ISBN: 978-0-367-60590-2 (pbk)

Typeset in Times New Roman
by Taylor & Francis Books

David G. Gliddon dedicates this book to his mother, Doris E. Gliddon. William J. Rothwell dedicates this book to his wife Marcelina V. Rothwell, his son Froilan Perucho, his daughter Candice Szczesny, his grandsons Aden and Gabriel, and his granddaughter Freya.

Contents

viii *Contents*

Figures

Contributors

Debra (Keppy) Arnoldsen is a retired Instructor of Biology from Penn State University, USA, with a 1995 Master of Science degree. In 2011, she became an inventor and entrepreneur in anaerobic digester technology. Her research interests include nutrient acquisition from food wastes and fertilizer efficiency.

Norma Nusz Chandler is a lecturer in Construction Management Program at South Dakota State University, Brookings, SD, USA. She obtained her DM in Environmental and Social Sustainability from Colorado Technical University in 2014. Her research interests include community, building, and infrastructure sustainability including corrosion and safety. norma.nuszchandler@gmail.com

Wesley E. Donahue is Associate Professor of Management Development and Education at Penn State. He is a registered professional engineer, six-sigma black belt, and has co-authored the book *Creating In-house Sales Training and Development Programs*, as well as a host of other education and training materials. wed105@psu.edu

Mike Erdman is the Walter Robb Director of Engineering Leadership Development and Instructor of Engineering Science at Pennsylvania State University, USA. He received his BS in Engineering Science, MS in Mechanical Engineering from USC, and studied at the Rensselaer Polytechnic Institute. He was a manager of technology development for GE and Lockheed Martin. ame17@psu.edu

Jonathan Gangi is Assistant Professor of Music & Arts Entrepreneurship and Founding Director of the Arts Entrepreneurship program at Pennsylvania State University, USA. His research is published in several arts management and arts entrepreneurship journals. His research interests include arts entrepreneurship, management, and innovation leadership. jjg27@psu.edu

David G. Gliddon is Lead Faculty in the College of Business and Management at Colorado Technical University, USA. He earned his doctorate and undergraduate degrees from Penn State University, USA, and his Master's degree from the University of Scranton, USA. As part of his post-doctoral work, he earned certificates from MIT, Yale, and the University of Cambridge, UK. As a member of the White House Community Leaders program, Dr. Gliddon attended a White House briefing and met President Barack Obama and First Lady Michelle Obama at a White House reception. Dr. Gliddon's work has inspired the development of innovation leadership programs, writings, and awards throughout the world in governments, universities, businesses, and popular media. dr.gliddon@gmail.com

Meg Handley is the Associate Director of Engineering Leadership Outreach at Pennsylvania State University, USA. She obtained her PhD in Workforce Education from Penn State University in 2017. Her research interests include engineering leadership, emotional intelligence, and career development. mhh11@engr.psu.edu

Catherine Haynes is a retired US Army Human Resources Manager. She obtained a dual PhD in Human Resources/Organizational Development and in Comparative and International Education from Pennsylvania State University, USA. Her research interest includes Roles of Indigenous Tour Guides in Providing Authentic Experiences for Guided in the Caribbean. cathy7830@gmail.com

Kathryn Jablokow is Professor of Engineering Design and Mechanical Engineering at the Pennsylvania State University, USA. She obtained her PhD in Electrical Engineering from the Ohio State University in 1989. Her research interests include design cognition, engineering creativity, invention, and high performance design teams. kwl3@psu.edu

Maureen Connelly Jones has taught in higher education for over 20 years in both health policy and administration and nursing and has been in the healthcare industry for over 25 years. Her research identifies CEO characteristics as they lead through crisis by conducting interviews with the CEOs and members of their executive team in an effort to building a competency model for selection. She has published in the areas of organization development and change, evaluation of change, succession planning, talent management, and leadership innovation. Maureen@psu.edu

Juliette Kleinmann is a senior financial professional with over 20 years of financial expertise in the USA. She obtained her Doctorate of Management from Colorado Technical University in 2016. Her research interests include financial forensics, fraud interrogation and terrorism funding. Dr.JD. Kleinmann@gmail.com

Frank Theodore Koe is Associate Professor of Engineering Entrepreneurship at Pennsylvania State University, USA. Frank's research and writing interests lie in innovation, entrepreneurship, intrapreneurship, and textile technology. The Second Edition of his text, *Fabric for the Designed Interior* was recently published by Bloomsbury. ftkoe5561@gmail.com

Dena Lang is the Associate Director of the Engineering Leadership Research at Pennsylvania State University, USA. She obtained her PhD in Biomechanics from Penn State University in 2003. Her research interests include quantitative genetics of skeletal tissue mechanics, behavior and the indoor environment, and engineering leadership. tcl133@psu.edu

Patricia Macko is a PhD candidate at Pennsylvania State University, USA. She is obtaining her PhD with an emphasis in Workforce Education and Development. She has published in several journals and is chapter author in several published books. Her research interests include Talent Development, Competencies, and Learning Technologies. pem146@psu.edu

Ward E. Marshall is a retired United States Army Colonel. His tours of duty include the Army Staff Pentagon, Advisor to Afghan National Security Forces and Nation Iraqi Army Advisor. He obtained a Doctorate of Management with Homeland Security emphasis from Colorado Technical University. wardmarshall2012@yahoo.com

Jong Gyu Park is a PhD candidate in the Workforce Education and Development program at the Pennsylvania State University, USA. Prior to studying at Penn State, he was a management consultant at Deloitte and Willis Towers Watson. His research interests include team leadership and leadership development in the organization. pjk228@gmail.com

Walter Robb graduated from Penn State in 1948, joined GE in 1951, and retired as CTO in 1993. He led the company's development of the gold standard CT and MRI Scanners. In retirement, he has assisted 20 different start-ups and published a book entitled *Taking Risks*. In 1994, he received the National Medal of Technology.

William J. Rothwell, Ph.D., SPHR, SHRM-SCP, CPLP Fellow is President of Rothwell & Associates, Inc. and Rothwell & Associates, LLC. He is also a Professor-in-Charge of the Workforce Education and Development program, Department of Learning and Performance Systems, at Pennsylvania State University, University Park campus. He has authored, co-authored, edited, or co-edited 300 books, book chapters, and articles – including over 90 books. He has also worked as a consultant for over 40 multinational corporations, including Motorola China, General Motors, Ford, and many others. In 2012 he earned ASTD's prestigious Distinguished Contribution to Workplace Learning and Performance Award, and in 2013 ASTD honored him by naming him as a Certified Professional in Learning and Performance (CPLP) Fellow. In 2014 he was given the Asia-Pacific International Personality Brandlaureate Award. He was the first US citizen named a Certified Training and Development Professional (CTDP) by the Canadian Society for Training and Development in 2004. wjr9@psu.edu

R. Lee Viar IV is a Professor of Business and Management, working with students online and on campus in the USA. After earning his PhD in Post-

Secondary Adult Education and Training in 2007, he has completed post-doctoral studies at Harvard, Vanderbilt, MIT, University of Oklahoma, and Norwich University. His publications and research focus on the challenges of the adult learner and corresponding issues. general1865@myactv.net

Acknowledgements

Cassandra, Eric, and the families, colleagues, and friends of the editors and chapter authors. Friar and Rin. The administration, faculty, students, and alumni at Colorado Technical University and Penn State University. Kristina, Laura, Matthew, Kris and all the staff at Routledge. Thank you all for your support!

Foreword

In this book, we will explore innovation leadership. Innovation is one of the most important success factors in modern businesses and society. The importance of human innovation can be traced back to our time as hunters and gatherers when we began to use early tools as primitive technologies. These tools became one of our first human innovations. At some point, people decided to develop civilization, live in groups, and survive together in communities, another significant innovation. As these communities began to trade with one another, early innovations in business, such as simple currencies, began to develop. Early peoples explored, established trade routes, and discovered new ideas and cultures.

By our very nature, people create. We build, we design, we draw, we harmonize, we dance, we help, we protect, we plant, we study, we discover, and we write. When we look at the world around us, it is filled with innovations now and from our past. Like the pyramids of Egypt, historical innovations are a great source of study, inspiration, and awe, when defining human potential. When Johannes Gutenberg applied his skills as a blacksmith to create movable type and the modern printing press, he created an innovation that enlightened society. People were able to learn and be inspired by writings that drove our ability to create in many different disciplines across many different cultures. In this same spirit, the internet has created an interconnected society.

People like Johannes Gutenberg are innovation leaders. They are those imaginative people that help to develop and communicate new ideas. No matter how big or how small, if it is useful, the innovation may help to support progress in society. There are innovation leaders in all walks of life, and in this book, we will describe best practices that can be used to support innovation leadership. The book is organized in two parts. In Part I, we discuss the basic concepts of innovation leadership such as the CREATE Model of Innovation Leadership, the competencies of innovation leaders, followership, synergy in innovation network teams, building a culture of continuous innovation, and funding innovations. In Part II of the book, we describe innovation leadership success stories in the arts, the private sector, education, sustainability, cultural relations, agriculture, the public sector, and health care.

Many early explorers set out on their journeys to discover new trade routes, even discovering America along the way! They helped to establish the foundation for the modern global economy. Entrepreneurs rely on innovation in order to create new businesses. Likewise, many non-profit organizations rely on innovation in order to support their cause. Artists rely on innovation for expression. Corporations rely on innovations to grow or improve performance. Thus, innovation remains an important part of the modern economy for an organization's growth, cultural development, or survival. More importantly, it is an important part of humanity. On behalf of the editors and chapter authors of this book, we hope you enjoy exploring innovation leadership.

Dr. David G. Gliddon

Part I
Innovation leadership theory

1 Defining and practicing innovation leadership using the CREATE Model

David G. Gliddon

Imagine looking at a building made entirely of clear glass and watching what employees do in real time for an entire day. You might see them typing, talking on a phone, meeting, performing, presenting, building, moving supplies, designing with technology, operating machinery, completing sales, supporting customers, practicing, or interacting globally. Each of these activities happens simultaneously in real-time coordinating hundreds or even thousands of people to keep an organization running smoothly. People are the organization. If we focus on the individuals in an organization of people and discover the whole creative person in a role, it can illuminate how truly innovative that organization can be.

An innovation is a new idea or an idea perceived as new that creates progressive change. Innovation leadership involves synthesizing different leadership styles in organizations to influence employees to produce creative ideas, products, services and solutions. It is a practice and an approach to change management (Gliddon, 2009). Groups, teams, organizations, and governments can implement innovation leadership to support the development of innovations (Gliddon, 2012). There are many leadership, management, change, communication, and educational theories commonly used in innovation leadership and many will be explored throughout this book.

Description

Leaders inspire their followers to achieve a shared goal (Garrett, 2014). The key role in the practice of innovation leadership is that of the innovation leader. Within an organization, people develop creative ideas that can become innovations. Creativity is a common human inspiration and innovation leaders can inspire their followers by encouraging creativity. An innovation leader collaboratively develops a new idea with creative employees and key stakeholders and makes it real (Gliddon, 2013).

The CREATE Model is a model of innovation leadership that includes a set of steps that innovation leaders can use to develop and diffuse an innovation and create progressive change. It is synthesized from a triangulated set of theories including the action research model, path-goal theory, and leader

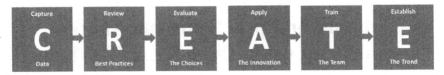

Figure 1.1 Gliddon's CREATE Model of innovation leadership

member exchange theory. There are six steps in The CREATE Model of innovation leadership (see Figure 1.1).

The CREATE Model can be used by an innovation leader with a group, team, or organization whose goal is to innovate. In the following paragraphs, each step of The CREATE Model will be described.

Capture Data: Capture applicable organizational data sources and/or conduct data gathering activities. Data is at the heart of an innovation since the new ideas are inspired greatly by a vision for the future using a clear assessment of the past and present. Analyzing both quantitative data and qualitative data sheds light on the scale of innovation and also the potential for consumers of the innovation. The variety and type of analyses is commonly dependent on the nature of the innovation. However, some common methods of data analysis such as surveys, focus groups, observations, interviews, needs analysis, emergent group behavior analysis, quality assessments, performance measurements, and customer service data can help support a strong foundation of data for the development of an innovation.

Review Best Practices: Review applicable best practices that exist within the organization or in the external organizational, market, or customer environment. Best practices in organizations are valued much like experience is valued in employees. The step of reviewing best practices helps innovation leaders to avoid developing innovations that fundamentally may take an organization in the wrong direction. Likewise, the best practices help to build a foundation for new ideas. Knowing what works can help to drive variations on or a synthesis of good ideas.

Evaluate the Choices: Evaluate the choices using the information gathered as well as any inspired ideas when capturing data and reviewing best practices. Knowing what *is* helps to drive knowing what *can be*. Knowing the choices can help innovation leaders to determine how the innovation might work, what the innovation might do, and how ideas can be combined to develop an innovation. This stage can include a wide variety of interactions including: planning/strategy meetings, brainstorming sessions, collaboration using technologies, and discussions. Key stakeholders, creative employees, and innovation leaders build innovations as they thoroughly evaluate the choices and develop a goal for the innovation.

Apply the Innovation: Apply the innovation in a test environment. In this step, the innovation is engineered or created and rigorously tested to ensure that it meets its intended goal. This may include developing multiple prototypes for the innovation to discover which may be most feasible, efficient, or productive. During this period, the innovation may be refined or tweaked depending upon the changing nature of the organization, regulatory approval, or its business environment. Again, it is critical that the innovation leader involve key stakeholders and creative employees in a collaborative discussion regarding the innovation to gain approval for the larger scale implementation of an innovation.

Train the Team: Once the innovation has passed the test environment and is approved, it is now ready for broader implementation. The production team (anyone needed to produce, diffuse, and implement the innovation on its full scale) should be trained on the innovation and how it is to be produced, used, and managed. Educating people using effective training methods on the innovation is critical to building a positive reception. Since innovations are new ideas, they may not initially be easily understood. To help people understand the nature of an innovation, it is important to relate it to concepts that exist and then explain how the innovation differs in nature.

Establish the Trend: Establish the trend to support the diffusion of the innovation. Launch, communicate, and market the innovation to users. Effectively marketing an innovation provides users with the knowledge they need to choose to adopt the innovation. Getting innovators, early adopters, opinion leaders, and change agents initially on board with the innovation plays a critical part in the diffusion process. Since diffusion is a social process, preparing a strong communication plan between the organization and the community of users including support for feedback, user support, building continued excitement and continuous quality improvement for the innovation can greatly enhance the reception of the innovation.

Research foundations

The CREATE Model of innovation leadership, when used by an innovation leader and applied in a group, team, or organization can support the development of innovations. To understand why organizations may choose to develop innovations we will explore the types of innovations, the sources of innovations, levels of innovations, and the purposes of innovations. There are two types of innovations. Exploratory innovation involves generating brand new ideas, Value-added innovation involves modifying and improving ideas that already exist (Adjei, 2013). There is a conceptual relationship between the sources, levels, and purposes of innovations (see Figure 1.2).

The creative minds behind the most significant innovations in our society are influenced by many different sources. Creative ideas are mental constructs that have been experienced by an individual. By using analytical thinking and inspiration, our minds combine the useful attributes from these constructs and create an innovation. The innovation can then be shared as a group level innovation or for development as an organization level or market level innovation. If the innovation is widely diffused it becomes a societal level innovation. However, the innovation can typically be traced to an individual level or group level

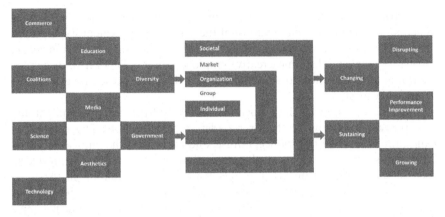

Figure 1.2 Sources, levels, and purposes of innovations

innovation (Gliddon, 2013). An innovation at the group or individual level can be characterized as stemming from the following sources.

Commerce: Businesses, financial trends, and economic performance provide influences by which the generation of innovations is necessary. Although focus is usually placed upon market and organization level innovations, these influences have profound impact on the individual, their inspiration, and career. In this light, commerce creates and atmosphere of competition in the market for organizations, and in obtaining jobs for individuals. Commercial sales are driven by advertising which heavily influences our society using a variety of forms of media as a primary vehicle for their message. Within an organization, the focus of a performance management or evaluation system is to use financial rewards, such as bonuses and raises, or intrinsic rewards such as promotions with better pay to motivate groups and individuals. In striving for these rewards, individuals and groups generate innovations to stay competitive (Hirshleifer, 1994).

Coalitions: Coalitions are groups or organizations that are formed to promote or discourage an ideal or practice. They are active participants in political discussion and can have much power to make political decisions. With this power comes a significant voice in the decision to adopt innovations. Likewise, because coalitions typically have competitive coalitions that oppose an ideal or practice, they compete for the power to make decisions. The choice for individuals, groups, or organizations to align with a coalition is influenced by their values and attitudes shaping their perspectives and creative thoughts (Barrett, 2000).

Science: Scientific discoveries have profoundly shaped the lives of our global community. With each new discovery comes more knowledge about our world, our health, and our universe. As discoveries are made, they shape our creative thinking and allow scientists to develop medical treatments, environmental safeguards, and new technologies. The impact of these discoveries is profound from the life-saving power of pharmaceuticals to the exploratory power of space probes. The innovations generated though the foundations of science may lay a groundwork for commercial market success for the organizations that support their development. Many coalitions have arisen because of the agreement or disagreement with the ethics of developing and commercializing scientific discoveries (Westwood, 1988).

Technology: A technology is a tool that can be used to assist an individual or group of individuals with a task. The simple technologies of our ancestors such as wheels and stone carved knives have developed into the highly intricate and complex devices that have combined significant scientific discoveries with practical use to create societal level innovations. Innovations using new technologies have changed our society and made our lives, in many cases, safer, more secure, and have provided an adequate level of convenience. Technology has a profound impact on commerce and the innovations in technology have both driven our economy and allowed businesses to be carried out much more efficiently (Damanpour, 1996).

Education: We seek education to learn something new about a topic of our interest. Learning is a constant human activity and is not merely confined to lectures, reading, or classrooms. We learn to keep abreast of the news, to find a time to go to the movies, discover new philosophies, to support the lives of our friends and family, capitalize on a great sale, and efficiently complete tasks on the job. Learning is a significant precursor to innovation, and the institutions that complete research and provide education impact our perspectives in a profound way. Likewise, our own individual learning pursuits in libraries, the internet, and in communities support the generation of innovations. As each person is unique, they provide a unique perspective on the knowledge they have gained and through analytical thinking or discussions with those in their social network can support the diffusion of innovations. In order for an innovation to make an impact, we must first learn or be educated about it in some way (Buckler, 1996).

Media: To communicate an innovation, it must be placed in some form of media. There are many useful forms of media such as books, magazines, journals, emails, web sites, television, movies, apps, and text messages. The message that is conveyed and the form by which it is conveyed in media can influence an individual's creative thoughts and assist in generating innovations. The term 'the media' refers to those who report and discuss the news or current issues. However, not all forms of media are highly credible and some can be severely biased by commercial and political coalitions. When viewing media, a cautious sense of objectivity should be maintained. A critical problem with the diffusion of innovations in the media is the evaluation of the innovation's usefulness in concert with the forces that may be promoting it for solely commercial or political purposes (Gazi, 2014).

Aesthetics: The artistic, musical, literary, theatrical, and motion picture works of individuals within our society provide inspiration for innovation. When we experience the aesthetic, it can impact our thoughts, feelings, and provide unconscious answers to questions that we may not be able to understand consciously. In many pieces of literature, we relate our lives or situations to stories, poetry, or writings that can provide guidance or help us to think creatively. In art, we see expressions that can encourage our imaginative abilities or develop a connection to a culture. In music, we find energy, solace, imagination or motivation that provides a sense of synergistic creativity. In motion pictures and theatrical experiences, we find a recreation of a fictional or non-fictional reality. Our society is greatly impacted by the aesthetic; it serves as a cultural symbol of our creativity (George, 2016b).

Diversity: In our world, there are countless cultures, subcultures, and religions that have developed through various points in history. The culture or religion that an individual or group of individuals belongs to has a significant impact on their values, attitudes, and expressions. Unfortunately, much of the conflict that we see in the world today is based upon an ignorance of or rejection of the practices and beliefs of different cultural or religious groups. What is missed in this conflict is the impact that understanding and appreciating these cultures and religions can have on the generation of innovations. Sharing and celebrating our cultures and religions can promote the generation of innovations and peace (King, 1999).

Government: The method by which a nation of people is governed can greatly impact their society, market, organizations, groups, and individuals. As government is closely linked with political coalitions, many of the decisions made to adopt innovations are ultimately decided in public discussion. Similarly, once an innovation has been discussed, government funding and support can provide much motivation to diffuse the innovation throughout our society. The military and police forces of many governments support the research and development of innovations for the security and protection of its people and resources (Pellerin, 2017). In a global context, leaders and diplomats representing governments can discuss and diffuse innovations generated in their country for the use of other world populations.

There are five levels of innovations: (a) the societal level, (b) the market level, (c) organization level, (d) the group level, and (e) the individual level. At the societal level, innovations have a profound impact. The innovation can reach the societal level if it has been widely diffused and adopted. Innovations can influence the thoughts and opinions of masses of people and can cause those masses to mobilize around the idea to create change. A market level innovation is primarily focused on increasing the market share of a company though increased sales of a product or service. Market level innovations are the focus of many businesses in their quest to stay competitive or increase profit. However, as not all innovations are viewed positively by consumers, innovations can backfire and reduce market share, profit, and an organization's competitiveness. This highlights the great risk involved in generating and promoting market level innovations and the need for thorough evaluation and discussion of the potential of an innovation (Pisano, 2015).

An organization level innovation aims to improve an organization's overall performance. This can be accomplished as employees generate innovations to improve processes, develop management practices, fine-tune fiscal strategies, generate new business models, or implement new technologies. Many of an organization's best practices are produced by organization level innovations. Once adopted, these innovations may provide the organization with a greater level of performance which can potentially translate into growth or higher profit (Damanpour, 1991).

Group level innovations are much like a seed pod. It is in groups that many individuals feel comfortable generating innovations by brainstorming or piggy-backing ideas together. Once the innovation has been recognized by the group, it can be discussed, evaluated, and developed for use at the organization level or market level. A common example of group level innovation is the work of a new product team. A new product team is typically cross functional with members from many different departments. This kind of team is tasked with using group level innovations to create a market level innovation that can potentially increase market share. Another example of group level innovation is a process improvement team. This group is tasked with using group level innovations to create an organization level innovation that can improve the productivity of the organization's employees (Gardner, 2002).

It is from our own minds that innovations flow. The focus at the individual level is thinking creatively. The most useful innovations in an organization can be generated by any employee at any moment for any reason. However, it is important to understand what has influenced the creative thoughts of that employee in order to be able to understand their innovation. As an innovation leader, it is also useful to explore the influences on creative employees in order to help develop the creative thinking skills of other employees (Oliver, 2015).

In order to be useful, an innovation needs a purpose. Generating innovations without predefined purpose can be a fruitful raw experience of creativity, but a purpose at some point should emerge from the creative minds of those generating the innovation. It should have practical significance at one of the levels of innovation discussed above. More clearly, an innovation has to do something realistically progressive for a group of people and change some aspect of their life or work practices (Tucker, 2017).

Changing: Innovations are commonly linked with change in organizations. Although organizational change can be challenging because of strong resistance to change, it is a reality that many organizations must face to stay competitive. Evolutionary change occurs incrementally over time and is focused narrowly on some distinct aspect of the organization. For example, many organizations strive to make their customer service practices more user-friendly for consumers. Over time, a company may implement innovations that can improve the quality, efficiency and friendliness of their customer service department. Revolutionary change occurs when an organization wants to entirely change its business practices, technology, or processes. The revolution in this change is broad in focus and its innovations are a radical departure from its previous state (Lewis, 1993).

Sustaining: Many times, maintaining competitiveness in a market or within an organization means keeping pace with competitors. Innovations may be directed toward sustaining the organization's status in the market, its processes, or some other aspect that has historically been a standard. When sustaining, innovations are used to augment what already exists in the organization to improve it in some way or to update a current practice, process, or product that has deteriorated. The improvements made by sustaining innovations provide an organization with a clear path for progress that builds on established products, practices, and processes (Quinn, 2016).

Disrupting: In order to provide a competitive advantage, an organization or group may want to use innovations to challenge the success of a current competitive product or service in order to focus consumers on a new product or service. This represents a radical departure from preexisting products, services, or products, and is designed to bring attention to a new market level innovation. The term 'disruptive innovation' has been used to characterize this function of an innovation. Disruptive innovations are commonly associated with technological products and can replace current technologies with new technologies that are more efficient or provide more value to customers (Spahr, 2015).

Performance Improvement: In order for an organization, group, or individual to raise performance it may require a performance improvement innovation. Performance is characterized in organizations as completing tasks with more efficiency based upon an increased level of job knowledge or helpful technology. Performance, however is also linked to athletic, musical, and theatrical improvement. A performance improvement innovation for a sports team may be a new play or technique. In musical and theatrical productions, a performance improvement innovation may be new methods of practice or technologies such as lighting and sound that create a significant impact upon an audience (George, 2016a).

Growing: Innovations can also be used for supporting the growth of an organization. Many organizations who are not focused on profit may find that growth is a mission in order to enhance the organization's offerings for all members. Growth also can mean an increased level of impact upon a societal issue, learning community, or social activity. At the individual level, growth innovations may be associated with the development of an individual's knowledge, skills, abilities, or competencies. In science, growth innovations can be used to develop new ways of exploring the galaxy (Kuczmarski, 1996).

Application and implementation strategies

There are three perspectives that are useful when exploring innovation leadership: (a) the interactive process, (b) the individual, and (c) the structural phenomenon (Slappendel, 1996). The interactive process perspective, as characterized by Roger's (1995) diffusion of innovations theory, describes diffusion as a means to communicate an innovation among others within a social system. Although this can be done using a wide variety of media ranging from a global marketing campaign to word of mouth conversations, many technologies such as email, video, and social and professional networking platforms or a combination of these methods are commonly used to diffuse innovations.

The individualist perspective focuses on the characteristics of innovation leaders. One practical way to explore the characteristics of innovation leaders is to understand an innovation leader's competencies. A competency is a common measure used in organizations to ensure that an employee has both the knowledge and knowhow to do their job (Rothwell, 2011). A competency model is used as part of a job description to select, train, and evaluate the performance of an innovation leader. Many organizations have developed the role of an innovation leader as a unique job or have incorporated portions of the role of an innovation leader in various jobs. Thus, applying the competency model of innovation leaders in these key strategic roles in an organization is a critical part of using innovation leadership in organizations (Gliddon, 2006). In Chapter 2 of this book, the competency model of innovation leaders will be presented.

The structural phenomenon perspective focuses on how an organization's structure can be adapted to be suitable to develop innovations. Some examples include process reengineering, policy development, strategic partnerships, mergers/acquisitions, and building a culture of innovation. A cross functional innovation network team can be developed to support creating new products, processes, programs, or to do pure research and development. In many organizations, common innovation leadership networks include teams or groups in business development, sales, marketing, human resources, research, product development, information technology, design, communications, and finance. Likewise, cross-functional or product development teams are common innovation leadership networks. These teams or groups are commonly tasked with discovery, creativity, and producing innovations (Roffe, 1999).

Discussion

Innovation leadership using the CREATE Model provides a method by which innovation can be coordinated and led within and between groups and organizations to focus their efforts and increase their ability to innovate. An innovation leader, using the CREATE Model applies their competence to develop a culture of innovation within an organization. What is highly advantageous about the model of innovation leadership is that it is applicable to many organizations, not merely for-profit corporations. Non-profit, community, athletic, religious, artistic, musical, or political organizations can derive much benefit from incorporating the model of innovation leadership. Likewise, it is broadly applicable to many industries and institutions. In Part II of the book, innovation leadership success stories will be presented that describe how innovation leaders have successfully used innovations to drive success, growth, and progress in many different types of instances.

The book primarily focuses on the individual perspective of innovation leadership. However, there are currently multiple perspectives on the definition of what an innovation leader truly is. An individual in an organization, a group within an organization, the organization itself, and even a community, state, or nation can be considered an innovation leader. Although there are differing perspectives on how to frame innovation leaders in this fashion, within each frame is the individual in an organization responsible for the development and diffusion of innovations (Massar, 2017). Therefore, even though we may call nations, states, organizations, or groups innovation leaders, it is still most critical to assess the individual innovation leader or innovation leaders that are driving innovation leadership within each frame.

Summary

Leaders inspire their followers to achieve a shared goal. The key role in the practice of innovation leadership is that of the innovation leader. Within an organization, people develop creative ideas that can become innovations. Creativity is a common human inspiration and innovation leaders can inspire their followers by encouraging creativity. An innovation leader collaboratively develops a new idea with creative employees and key stakeholders and makes it real. The CREATE Model is a model of innovation leadership that includes a set of steps that innovation leaders can use to develop and diffuse an innovation and create progressive change. There are six steps in The CREATE Model of innovation leadership including: Capture Data, Review Best Practices, Evaluate the Choices, Apply the Innovation, Train the Team, and Establish the Trend. There are two types of innovations: exploratory and value-added. There are five levels by which to understand innovations including: the societal level, the market level, the organization level, the group level, and the individual level. The sources of innovation include: commerce, coalitions, science, technology, education, media, aesthetics, diversity, government. Innovations have a purpose or function including: changing, sustaining, disrupting, performance improvement and growing. There are three perspectives that are useful when ensuring innovation leadership is applied in an organization: the interactive process, the individual, and the structural phenomenon. What is highly advantageous about the model of innovation leadership is that it is applicable to many organizations, industries, and institutions.

References

Adjei, D, 2013, 'Innovation leadership management', *International Journal of ICT and Management*, vol. 1, no. 2, pp. 103–106.

Barrett, FJ, and Peterson, R, 2000, 'Appreciative learning cultures: Developing competencies for global organizing', *Organization Development Journal*, vol. 1, no. 2, pp. 10–22.

Buckler, B, 1996, 'A learning process model to achieve continuous improvement and innovation', *The Learning Organization*, vol. 3, no. 3, pp. 31–35.

Damanpour, F, 1991, 'Organizational innovation: A meta-analysis of effects of determinants and moderators', *Academy of Management Journal*, vol. 34, no. 3, pp. 555–591.

Damanpour, F, 1996, 'Organizational complexity and innovation: Developing and testing multiple contingency models', *Management Science*, vol. 42 no. 5, pp. 693–717.

Garrett, SL, 2014, *Pure Heart Thoughts: An Approach to Authentic Leadership*, CreateSpace, Seattle, WA.

Gardner, L, and Stough, C, 2002, 'Examining the relationship between leadership and emotional intelligence in senior level managers', *Leadership & Organization Development Journal*, vol. 23, no. 1, pp. 68–79.

Gazi, AI and Alam, AA, 2014, 'Leadership, efficacy, innovations and their impacts on productivity', *ASA University Review*, vol. 8, no. 1, pp. 253–262.

George, B, 2016a, 'Innovation leaders create long-term value', *Huffington Post*. Available at http://www.huffingtonpost.com/bill-george/innovation-leaders-create_b_9626336.html [Accessed 25 Aug. 2017]

George, B, 2016b, 'The leadership quality that truly separates Disney's Bob Iger from his peers', *Fortune*, Available at http://fortune.com/2016/04/04/the-leadership-quality-that-truly-separates-disneys-bob-iger-from-his-peers/ [Accessed 25 Aug. 2017].

Gliddon, DG, 2006, 'Forecasting a competency model for innovation leaders using a modified Delphi technique.' PhD. The Pennsylvania State University.

Gliddon, DG, 2009, 'Performance management systems', In D. Leigh and R. Watkins, Eds, *Handbook for the Selection and Implementation of Human Performance Technologies*, ISPI/Jossey Bass, San Francisco, CA.

Gliddon, DG, 2012, 'Innovation leadership is a key ingredient to business success', *Colorado Technical University*. Available at: http://www.coloradotech.edu/resources/blogs/december-2012/innovation-leadership [Accessed 25 Aug. 2017].

Gliddon, DG, 2013, 'Toward a model of innovation leadership', Proceedings of the 16th Annual ANTSHE National Conference, ANTSHE, Hagerstown, MD.

Hirshleifer, J, Jensen, MC, Hall, RE, Shleifer, A, and Meckling, WH, 1994, 'Economics and organizational innovation', *Contemporary Economic Policy*, vol. 12, no. 2, pp. 1–21.

King, S, and Nicol, DM, 1999, 'Organizational enhancement through recognition of individual spirituality: Reflections of Jacques and Jung', *Journal of Organizational Change Management*, vol. 12, no. 3, pp. 234–242.

Kuczmarski, TD, 1996, 'What is innovation? The art of welcoming risk', *The Journal of Consumer Marketing*, vol. 13, no. 5, pp. 7–10.

Lewis, LK, and Seibold, DR, 1993, 'Innovation modification during intra-organizational adoption', *The Academy of Management Review*, vol. 18, no. 2, pp. 322–355.

Massar, C, and Johnson, C, 2017, 'Students become social innovation leaders', *Bloomberg*. Available at https://www.bloomberg.com/news/audio/2017-06-13/bloomberg-markets-students-become-social-innovation-leaders [Accessed 25 Aug. 2017].

Oliver, D, 2015, *Mantra Design: Innovate Buy or Die*, Xlibris, Bloomington, IN.

Pellerin, C, 2017, 'Defense innovation maintains military overmatch against adversaries', *U.S. Department of Defense*. Available at https://www.defense.gov/News/Article/Article/1172099/defense-innovation-maintains-military-overmatch-against-adversaries/ [Accessed 25 Aug. 2017].

Pisano, GP, 2015, 'You need an innovation strategy', *Harvard Business Review*. Available at https://hbr.org/2015/06/you-need-an-innovation-strategy [Accessed 25 Aug. 2017].

Quinn, B, 2016, 'Reframe to innovate: Recognizing you're an innovation leader', *Forbes*. Available at https://www.forbes.com/sites/brianquinn/2016/04/28/reframe-to-innovate-recognizing-youre-an-innovation-leader/#53eb881ab507 [Accessed 25 Aug. 2017].

Roffe, I, 1999, 'Strategic planning for the development of a training innovation', *Industrial and Commercial Training*, vol. 31, no. 5, pp. 163–177.

Rogers, EM, 1995, *Diffusion of Innovations*, The Free Press, New York.

Rothwell, WJ, 2011, *Invaluable Knowledge*, Amacom, New York.

Slappendel, C, 1996, 'Perspectives on innovation in organizations', *Organization Studies*, vol. 17 no. 1, pp. 107–130.

Spahr, P, 2015, 'What is innovative leadership? How imagination revolutionizes business', *St. Thomas University*. Available at http://online.stu.edu/innovative-leadership/ [Accessed 25 Aug. 2017].

Tucker, RB, 2017, 'Six innovation leadership skills everybody needs to master', *Forbes*. Available at www.forbes.com/sites/robertbtucker/2017/02/09/six-innovation-leadership-skills-everybody-needs-to-master/#40897d225d46 [Accessed 25 Aug. 2017].

Westwood, ARC, and Sekine, Y, 1988, 'Fostering creativity and innovation in an industrial R&D lab', *Research Technology Management*, vol. 31 no. 4, pp. 16–21.

2 The competencies of innovation leaders

Dena Lang, Meg Handley, and Kathryn Jablokow

Corporations are increasingly focused on using innovation leadership to develop their competitive edge. As a result, they are finding ways to harness the creativity of their employees in many different areas of their organizations including entrepreneurial and research and development programs. These programs require innovation leaders at multiple levels to serve in roles such as change champions, innovation team leaders, middle management sponsors, and executive leaders. Innovation leaders are critical for success at all levels of the organization and during all phases of the innovation process. This chapter will discuss general characteristics of an innovation leader during different steps of the CREATE model. Innovation leadership competencies and leadership styles will be discussed relative to the innovation environment and the characteristics of followers.

Description

Various leadership styles have been shown to be effective in specific organizational cultures and an organization's effectiveness has been shown to be partially dependent on its innovation leaders. For example, transformational leadership has been shown to be more effective for scientific R&D teams (Paulsen, 2013), because team members gain a sense of identity that leads to the adoption of more cooperative strategies (Paulsen, 2009). Individualists are more productive when working with transactional leaders, whereas collectivists are more productive working with a transformational leader (Jung, 1999). Therefore, innovation leaders must be able to adapt their leadership styles to match the culture and the type of employee. The previous chapter discussed the importance of different levels of innovations at the market level, organizational level, group level, and individual level. An analysis of effective innovation leadership within each of these levels can help to provide a framework through which the competencies of an innovation leader can be observed.

One purpose of a market level innovation is to impact the health and growth of the company. Market level innovations can also drive the emergence of a company. By focusing on market level innovations, innovation leaders can support strategic planning initiatives that help to maintain periods of growth and avoid decline. When an organization emerges, it focuses on establishing a vision for revolutionary change and generating new ideas that challenge the system. This period is full of uncertainty and chaos as the market innovation is being born. As the organization grows, there is increased focus on developing the capability to turn the market innovation into a successful product or service. Establishing an effective structure and building a culture of innovation is important during this period of the company's growth. Once the organization has established a viable market position, it can invest in business development and capitalize on growth opportunities. During this period, Vicere (1992) cautions that a focus on centralized decision-making and increased control systems can have both positive and negative effects on the organization. However, the key to an organization's survival is its ability to develop the flexibility to allow innovation leaders to operate at the emergence level to continually renew the organization.

Considering the organizational level, an innovation leader can focus on creating an organization that can consistently handle uncertainty. By consistently creating opportunities for more innovation, an organization opens itself up to more uncertainty as it diverts its resources to developing market level innovations. To facilitate this, innovation leaders can develop an organization that can adapt to maintain growth. Organic organizations may be better equipped to handle this type of uncertainty (Covin, 1990; Trott, 1998).

Innovation is all about people and innovation leaders need to recognize the importance of leading groups and developing individuals. They should foster employee creativity so that individuals can feel free to develop innovations. In many cases, innovations are the result of people solving problems. An effective innovation leader understands that people differ in their approach to solving problems. Kirton's Adaption-Innovation theory (2011) provides insight into individuals' preferred approaches to solving problems and illustrates how innovation leaders can use this information to impact the performance of teams and manage interpersonal relations based on these differences.

Kirton (2011) asserts that all humans are creative and solve problems, but our cognitive styles (our cognitive preferences for managing structure) differ from person to person. Kirton (2011) defines a continuum of cognitive style that extends from high Adaption (strong preference for more structure) on one end to high Innovation (strong preference for less structure) on the other end, with a full range of variations in between. People who are more adaptive tend to produce a sufficiency of ideas based more closely on, but stretching, existing agreed definitions of the problem and likely solutions. They prefer to analyze and develop these solutions in detail and proceed within the established theories, policies, and practices in their organizations. Much of their effort to change is focused on improving. In Kirton's (2011) model, people who are more innovative are more likely to reconstruct the problem in the pursuit of change. They are more comfortable separating the current problem from its enveloping accepted thought, paradigms, and customary viewpoints. They are more likely to emerge with a less expected and potentially radical solution, and they are less concerned with improving than with doing things differently. Neither general approach and thus no position along the cognitive style spectrum is ideal, with each having its own advantages and disadvantages, all of which is critical for an innovation leader to understand. This framework demonstrates the importance of knowing the people you are leading well enough to determine effective leadership strategies and styles to ensure success in problem-solving activities and leading innovation. Innovations create progressive change, making innovation leadership a practice and an approach to change management. In each of the levels discussed in this section, it is change that encourages the innovation leader to make decisions, evaluate organizational effectiveness, and adapt leadership styles to successfully lead innovation within the organization.

Research foundations

Innovation leaders play a critical role in facilitating the development of innovations in an organization. They are able to provide an environment that is conducive for creativity to spark innovations and to also support and guide innovation in groups (West, 2003). Their influence is critical in helping to bring an innovation to the implementation stage of the innovation process (Mumford, 2004). Mumford (2004) suggests that the ability of a leader to facilitate creativity and innovation is dependent on the characteristics of the leader, including their technical and professional expertise, as well as creative thinking skills. Mumford (2004) concluded that future research was needed to examine leadership in creative ventures, as previous models developed for routine settings could not simply be applied to creative/innovative ventures (Elkins, 2003; Govindarajan, 2005; Hamel, 2011; Teece, 2009).

In order to discuss the competencies of innovation leaders, we must first define some key terms. Characteristics are the underlying attributes of an individual that drive their behaviors. Behaviors are an individual's observable actions that are manifested as a result of the individual's characteristics (Spencer, 1993). A competency is an area of knowledge or skill that is critical when performing a job function; it includes both knowledge and expertise. Individual competencies are built from underlying characteristics that enable a person to demonstrate the competencies associated within a particular job (Boyatzis, 1982; Spencer, 1993). A competency model includes the set of competencies needed for effective performance (Bartram, 2005) in a particular role or position. The following paragraphs describe the competency model of innovation leaders organized into ten categories (see Figure 2.1) as identified by Gliddon (2006).

Learning: Individual learning, organizational learning, and knowledge management have all been linked to innovation. Individual learning increases an organization's knowledge base and can increase an innovation leader's effectiveness. An innovation leader is also critical in supporting an organizational culture that facilitates individual and organizational learning and effective

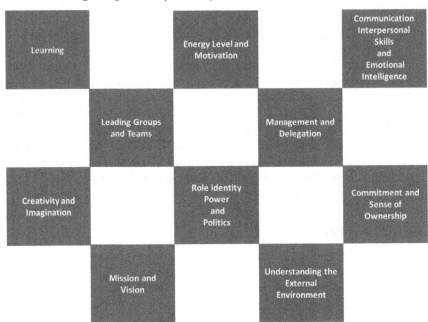

Figure 2.1 Gliddon's competency model of innovation leaders

knowledge management. Gliddon (2006) identified the following expert, core, and supplementary competencies related to Learning:

- Expert competency: identifies innovations.
- Core competencies: focuses on fundamentals, knowledge transfer, use of technical/professional expertise, curiosity, and business acumen.
- Supplementary competencies: conducts needs analysis, employs research methods, and values higher education.

Leading Groups and Teams: Once an innovation is identified, the ability to lead groups and teams is critical during innovation development, implementation, and adoption. Gliddon (2006) identified the following innovation leader competencies related to Leading Groups and Teams:

- Expert competencies: manages expectations and leads by example.
- Core competencies: knows the strengths and weaknesses of the team, teamwork, team commitment, empowerment, establishes team rapport, and team problem solving.
- Supplementary competency: cultivates loyalty.

Energy Level and Motivation: In order for the innovation leader to promote an innovation effectively and to lead groups and teams during innovation development, implementation, and adoption, they must understand their own motivations and understand how to motivate others, while maintaining the necessary energy level required to be successful. Gliddon (2006) identified the following competencies related to Energy Level and Motivation:

- Expert competency: sense of urgency.
- Core competencies: stress management, motivates others, ambition, passion driven, shows tenacity, and perseverance.
- Supplementary competencies: success driven and competitiveness.

Management and Delegation: The innovation leader must be able to manage resources effectively, including people, budgets, and time. Gliddon (2006) identified the following competencies associated with Management and Delegation:

- Expert competency: planning and project management.
- Core competencies: time management, encourages accountability, delegation, knows and utilizes resources, and balances team and individual priorities.

Communication, Interpersonal Skills, and Emotional Intelligence: To be effective, the innovation leader must have key interpersonal skills, well developed emotional intelligence, and be able to communicate their vision, seek support for the innovation, and direct followers through verbal, non-verbal, and written communication methods. Gliddon (2006) identified the following competencies related to Communication, Interpersonal Skills, and Emotional Intelligence:

- Core competencies: understands non-verbal cues, seeks to understand psyche of others, empathy, objectivity, fluency, translates literal speech, clarification, establishes feedback loops, addresses the correct audience, selects and uses appropriate communications, and asks open-ended questions.
- Supplementary competencies: exemplary writing skills, gate-keeping, open door policy, participates in active listening, tact, sparks discussion, and builds relationships.

Commitment and Sense of Ownership: For successful innovation, leaders must be personally committed to projects that require innovation (Cacioppe, 2000) and have a sense of ownership. Leaders need to develop a culture of trust and formulate challenging goals that are clearly linked to a work unit, the organization as a whole, as well as their customer, and they must ensure that individuals in their organization have meaningful work objectives and goals that are clearly connected to the goals of the organization and needs of the customer. Gliddon (2006) identified the following competencies related to Commitment and Sense of Ownership:

- Core competencies: takes responsibility, establishes a trust culture, goal setting, links corporate/department/team team goals, concern for customer, constantly seeks improvement, displays initiative, self-confidence, sets high standards, dedication, sense of pride, commitment to ethics, and develops focus.

- Supplementary competency: takes responsibility.

Creativity and Imagination: Innovation leaders must have an understanding of what creative employees value and be able to provide an environment that encourages new idea generation. The need for change often accompanies innovation, and the innovation leader must be a champion for change. Gliddon (2006) identified the following competencies related to Creativity and Imagination:

- Core competencies: identifies problems early, encourages new ideas, analytical thinking, champions change, eccentricity, flexibility, and generates new ideas.
- Supplementary competencies: accepts bad ideas, finds and uses analogues/benchmarks, employs brainstorming, builds visuals, employs alternate scenarios and role plays, takes time to muse, and risk-seeking.

Role Identity, Power, and Politics: The change that is often necessary to champion, develop, and implement innovation (whether the innovation is related to organizational processes or products and services) can initiate power struggles, as well as issues related to role identity, and can often lead to political challenges. Gliddon (2006) identified the following competencies related to Role Identity, Power, and Politics:

- Core competencies: integrity, professionalism, humility, negotiation, and impact and influence.
- Supplementary competencies: political savvy, salesmanship, employs game theory, diplomacy, and courage and conviction.

Mission and Vision: The successful innovation leader is able to develop, support, and articulate the organization's mission and vision, while aligning innovation efforts with the mission and vision. Gliddon (2006) identified the following competencies related to Mission and Vision:

- Core competencies: visionary leadership, strategy development, and encourages systems thinking.
- Supplementary competencies: employs multiple perspectives and organizational citizenship.

Understanding the External Environment: Bingham (2003) suggests that innovation leaders must have an understanding of the external environment in order to develop a successful business strategy. The external environment includes an organization's competitors and market, as well as relevant governmental policies and regulations. Gliddon (2006) identified the following competencies related to Understanding the External Environment:

- Core competency: knowledge of competitors.
- Supplementary competencies: organizational awareness, market and industry awareness, and cultivates cosmopolite relationships.

When using the competency model, the innovation leader may need to adjust his or her leadership style depending on the context in which they are operating. To be competitive, organizations have moved toward more inter-disciplinary team structures to be able to respond with agility and manage change rapidly (Rosen, 2011). Leaders of innovation teams must be able to overcome unique challenges of creative interdisciplinary teams to promote collaboration (Hunter, 2011) using appropriate leadership styles (Hemlin, 2013). Innovation leaders in middle management are often critical to ensuring that an innovation is not a victim of the corporate immune system. These leaders help champion the innovation by ensuring the innovation fits within the core business, justifying the innovation to reduce resistance, reducing risk by spreading risk, pacing risk, and reducing uncertainty, and helping to resolve potential conflicts by anticipating and answering potential objections and barriers within the existing business (Vincent, 2005). Corporate leader-ship must value, identify, support, and reward innovation sponsors within middle management to ensure the success of their innovation programs. Upper management leadership significantly influences both product/market innovations and organizational innovations, and this influence can be socio-culturally specific (Soken, 2014). To be effective, upper management must work to remove barriers to innovation and to establish and share norms and values that are consistent with the vision, mission, and strategy of the organization and that foster and support innovation (Elenkov, 2005).

Application and implementation strategies

This section will align the competency model of innovation leaders presented in the previous section with the stages of the CREATE model. One category in particular, Communication, Interpersonal Skills, and Emotional Intelli-gence, includes competencies that are essential across all phases of the CREATE Model. To some extent, all categories in the competency model may include competencies that are pertinent within each step of the CREATE Model. Gliddon's *Competency Assessment of Innovation Leaders* can be administered to employees and is an excellent way to develop innovation leaders. The following section highlights the competency model categories that are most pertinent to each phase of the CREATE model.

Capture Data: The innovation leader captures data from internal and external sources to understand the market and to provide information for new innovations. The competencies related to individual and organizational learning and knowledge management are important during the capture data stage of the CREATE model to ensure that the right innovations are being pursued in terms of the organization's expertise, mission, and vision, as well as the external environment, such as market conditions. Individual learning competencies relate to the ability of the innovation leader to identify appropriate innovations, drawing on their own curiosity, technical expertise and business acumen, and to their ability to effectively collect and evaluate the necessary information needed to make strategic business decisions. Successful innovation leaders keep up to date on market trends and they develop an information network, relying on the cultivation of external professional relationships that aid in the collection of data. In order to do this, the innovation leader must ensure that the organizational environment helps to facilitate organizational learning and knowledge management by supporting learning and development of their employees, experimentation, risk-taking, and a tolerance of failure. There are also many communication competencies that are critical to the innovation leader's ability to collect data from multiple sources, both internal and external to the company. The leader must also be able to cultivate a culture of trust and sense of loyalty to ensure that they are receiving honest input. This is often achieved through the implementation of ethical standards. As there is a direct link between competencies in the Learning category and the Mission and Vision and Understanding of the External Environment categories, during this step, the innovation leader must also have critical competencies in these two categories as well.

Review Best Practices: Benchmarking competitors or partners helps the innovation leader determine solutions that will best impact innovation development. These decisions require the motivation to want to improve, a commitment to improving, and an ability to think in unconventional ways to utilize benchmarking information for unique applications to lead innovation. This stage provides opportunities to unleash creative thinking based on the wealth of information coming in. During the Review Best Practices stage, the innovation leader must conduct an in-depth needs analysis to identify the strengths, weaknesses, opportunities and threats in their industry and organization. They must ensure that the organization has a well-defined mission and vision and be able to support and communicate the mission and vision effectively. The innovation leader's understanding of the external environment helps to ensure that the appropriate innovations are developed based on the strategic plans of the organization. They must have a solid understanding of their organization that comes from regular communication with various departments, including finance, accounting, and marketing, as well as investors. The innovation leader must keep up to date on market trends and have knowledge regarding how their competitors do business. The innovation leader must employ analytical thinking to identify critical issues, understand complex problems, generate varied solutions to the problems, and reflect on past performance to help guide future challenges.

Evaluate the Choices: This step requires the innovation leader to determine the choices at hand based on the data. Market level innovations may require a choice to embark on a value-added innovation for a current product or a disruptive innovation. Organizational level innovations may require adapting new processes, re-organizing, or implementing strategies to improve the organization. Whatever the team has discovered in previous steps, the innovation leader must identify and present the choices in a professional but influential manner, recognizing that these choices could represent significant change within the organization. Communication is key in this phase, as an innovation leader must provide appropriate communication based on the collected data and the benchmarking analysis.

Critical competencies needed in the Evaluate Choices stage can be found across many of the categories discussed above. The innovation leader must be able to anticipate the applicability of an innovation to the organization and have the business acumen to evaluate the strengths, weaknesses, opportunities, and threats associated with the innovation. To make informed choices, the innovation leader must be able to analyze and interpret the data collected in the previous stage and use their analytical problem solving skills to make informed choices. The innovation leader should participate in the development and implementation of the organization's long-term strategy. They should encourage and utilize systems thinking, capitalizing on their own value analysis and strategic planning skills. When making choices, the innovation leader must be able to identify the strengths of their team members, as well as the organization, in order to capitalize on those strengths and evaluate weaknesses that may need to be addressed. When evaluating choices, the innovation leader must be able to see beyond what is expected, with their sight set on the extraordinary, by understanding the difference between what is and what can be.

Apply the Innovation: This phase requires an innovation leader to form the best course of action in developing the innovation. It is here that the innovation leader faces uncertainty as the innovation is being developed and tested. In this step, it is important for organizations to be able to adapt to the needs of the innovation. An innovation leader needs to re-emphasize the commitment to the innovation and apply management principles as the innovation moves into a full-scale project. It is at this stage that the innovation leader can capitalize on their own technical and professional expertise to help influence the strategic direction of the innovation. They must be able to identify problems early, recognize that potential solutions may come from any level, and actively seek input from staff. Innovation leaders may learn that innovations are not easily making their way through highly controlled processes. When necessary, the innovation leader must be a champion for change. They should foster an environment that encourages team members to experiment with new ideas and enthusiastically support opportunities for process improvement. The innovation leader should possess humility and recognize that solutions may not be easily recognized or obtained; they cannot be afraid to seek advice from subordinates. As the innovation is applied, the innovation leader will often be tasked with resolving disputes and establishing agreement on actions to pursue and will need to depend on their negotiation skills to be successful.

The innovation leader may find that the individuals they are leading require different leadership strategies to make an impact in creative and problem-solving environments. In this stage, the innovation leader will rely on several competencies related to leading groups and teams. They must establish rapport with their team, communicating a shared vision, recognizing the value added by the team, and celebrating their successes. The innovation leader must be able to capitalize on the strengths of their team members, manage their expectations, and empower individuals to make decisions and the team to generate solutions. During this stage, the innovation leader must be able to establish a sense of urgency and be ambitious, passion driven, and have perseverance and tenacity. To be successful, the innovation leader should possess project management competencies, including planning, time management, and the ability to delegate, and effectively utilize available resources, encourage accountability, and balance team and individual priorities while motivating others. Communication competencies are key in successfully applying the innovation.

Train the Team: This stage moves from significant uncertainty to more structured processes, providing a level of certainty. The innovation, having passed pilot testing, moves into production, and marketing strategies are implemented. An innovation leader continues to rely on strong management and delegation techniques to manage the project, but also focuses on established team dynamics to ensure optimal environments for solving problems as the innovation moves out into the market. As the innovation moves from development to production, new problems may arise and new team members will be assigned. Many of the same competencies that were important during the Apply the Innovation stage are also important during the Train the Team stage. The innovation leader must once again anticipate and identify problems before they arise. They need to encourage the production team to provide input and utilize their problem-solving abilities to evaluate solutions. During this stage, the innovation leader may capitalize on their creativity by developing new approaches or systems that may be needed during production that either do not exist or are outside of their current experiences. They may also facilitate the creative processes of their peers and subordinates to do the same. The innovation leader must also champion any needed change, relying on their own flexibility, particularly concerning any needed process improvements. In this regard, they must rely on their own salesmanship to bring others on board in accepting the innovation and any needed changes in organizational processes by establishing credibility for the vision of the innovation.

The innovation leader must have a clear understanding of the strengths and weaknesses of the production team and address any needed training. They must establish a rapport with the team, manage the expectations of the team, and lead by example by matching their expectations for the team with their expectations of themselves. The innovation leader must empower individuals and team members to be able to make decisions in their areas of responsibility, while ensuring that everyone is contributing and engaged. They must clearly communicate a commitment to the team, as well as to the team's role in the organization. The innovation leader must maintain the sense of urgency and keep the team motivated. As was seen in the Apply the Innovation stage, all of the competencies in the management and delegation and communication categories are critical in the Train the Team stage of the CREATE model.

Establish the Trend: The innovation launches during this stage. A high level of energy and motivation should be sustained as the innovation enters the marketplace or is implemented within the organization. The innovation leader must continue to maintain a high level of energy and motivation, and be driven by passion, perseverance, and tenacity. They need to be success driven with a competitive nature to bring the innovation to fruition. The innovation leader must set challenging goals and constantly seek improvement. This is the stage where the innovation leader must maintain a commitment and sense of ownership toward the innovation. They need to assume personal responsibility for the innovation regardless of the outcome, displaying a long-term commitment and dedication to the organization. They must continue to monitor the external environment, including their competitors and the market, and continuously seek input from their customers. The innovation leader must maintain communications across departments and investors and be able to communicate the relationship between the team, department, and corporate goals and mission to maintain buy-in, commitment, and support for the innovation.

During the Establish the Trend stage, it is important for the innovation leader to utilize early adopters, opinion leaders, and change agents to help diffuse the innovation. It is in this stage that the innovation leader relies heavily on their ability to understand people, customers, their organization, and political environment to strategically plan an approach to influence the current moment. They must be politically savvy, be diplomatic (do not take 'no' for an answer), and show courage and conviction (be willing to put their job at risk if based on sound principles). Gaining support from early adopters, opinion leaders, and change agents is facilitated by the role identity of the innovation leader, including their professionalism and integrity. As with every other stage of the CREATE model, communication competencies are critical. The innovation leader must be able to effectively communicate their ideas and generate interest and support from others. They need to understand the psyche of others, including non-verbal cues, be active listeners, and ask questions. The innovation leader must be able to draw on their insights about other people's perspectives to formulate a communication strategy that will get others to support their ideas. They must be thoughtful in determining the most appropriate communication methods and timing, taking into consideration the impact at both the individual and organizational levels.

Discussion

There are a variety and number of competencies needed for an innovation leader to be successful and successful innovation leaders learn the importance of all these competencies as they develop (Menold, 2015). Take, for example, Jeff Bezos, CEO of Amazon, who focuses on Amazon being a company driven by experimentation (Gregersen, 2015). Bezos is an example of an innovation leader focused on being an individual learner, as well as creating a culture where organizational learning is a priority. Likewise, the CEO of UpWorks, Stephane Kasriel, identified as an introverted engineer, focuses on engaging employees through his personal development in emotional intelligence and by empowering technical people to influence the strategy of the company (Kasriel, 2016). Finally, Elon Musk, CEO of TESLA and SpaceX, is well known for his understanding of markets, continuous learning, and optimistic attitude (Mimaroglu, 2016). As an innovation leader, Musk tends to focus on learning, understanding external environments, and energy/motivation that drives optimism and perseverance. These real-world examples help to provide a picture of an innovation leader in action.

Summary

This chapter presented details of Gliddon's (2006) competency model of innovation leaders and aligned its categories with the stages of the CREATE model by identifying the competencies that are most pertinent in each step. Of all the categories in the competency model, the Communication, Inter-personal Skills, and Emotional Intelligence category appeared most frequently, highlighting its importance. The ability to communicate that knowledge, skill, and expertise, and to motivate others to act is paramount. Innovation leaders must have or obtain the insight to know which of the many competencies are needed in different situations. Insight is gained through observation and experience, making innovation leadership an 'active' pursuit. In other words, an innovation leader cannot simply sit and think about leadership; he or she must get out and 'do' leadership in order to gain the insights needed to move individuals, teams, and organizations forward. In combination, Gliddon's (2006) competency model for innovation leaders and the CREATE model of the innovation process provide a multi-level road map for innovation leaders to follow as they travel this path.

References

Bartram, D, 2005, *International Labour Migration: Foreign Workers and Public Policy.* New York: Palgrave MacMillan.
Bingham, P, 2003, 'Pursuing Innovation in a Big Organization', *Research Technology Management*, vol. 46, no. 4, 52–55.
Boyatzis, RE, 1982, *The Competent Manager: A Model for Effective Performance.* New York: John Wiley & Sons.

Cacioppe, R, 2000, 'Creating Spirit at Work: Re-visioning Organization Development and Leadership – Part 1', *Leadership & Organization Development Journal*, vol. 21, no. 1, pp. 48–55.

Covin, JG and Covin, T, 1990, 'Competitive Aggressiveness, Environmental Context, and Small Firm Performance', *Entrepreneurship: Theory and Practice*, vol. 14, no. 4, pp. 35–50.

Elenkov, DS and Manev, IM, 2005, 'Top Management Leadership and Influence on Innovation: The Role of Sociocultural Context', *Journal of Management*, vol. 31, no. 3, pp. 381–402.

Elkins, T and Keller, RT, 2003, 'Leadership in Research and Development Organizations: A Literature Review and Conceptual Framework', *Leadership Quarterly*, vol. 14, no. 4, p. 587.

Gliddon, DG, 2006, 'Forecasting a Competency Model for Innovation Leaders using a Modified Delphi Technique'. PhD. The Pennsylvania State University.

Govindarajan, V and Trimble, C, 2005, *10 Rules for Strategic Innovators; from Idea to Execution*, Boston: Harvard Business School Press.

Gregersen, H, 2015, 'The One Skill that Made Amazon's CEO Wildly Successful', Available at: http://fortune.com/2015/09/17/amazon-founder-ceo-jeff-bezos-skills/ [Accessed 25 Aug. 2017].

Hamel, G and Labarre, P, 2011, 'Improving our Capacity to Manage', *The Wall Street Journal Digital Networks US Edition*. Available at https://blogswsjcom/management/2011/04/06/improving-our-capacity-to-manage/ [Accessed 25 Aug. 2017].

Hemlin, S, Allwood, CM, Martin, BR, and Mumford, MD, 2013, *Creativity and Leadership in Science, Technology, and Innovation*. New York: Routledge.

Hunter, ST, Thoroughgood, CN, Myer, AT and Ligon, GS, 2011, 'Paradoxes of Leading Innovative Endeavors: Summary, Solutions, and Future Directions', *Psychology of Aesthetics, Creativity, and the Arts*, vol. 5, no. 1, pp. 54–66.

Jung, DI and Avolio, BJ, 1999, 'Effects of Leadership Style and Followers' Cultural Orientation on Performance in Group and Individual Task Conditions', *The Academy of Management Journal*, vol. 42, no. 2, pp. 208–218.

Kasriel, S, 2016, 'Upwork's CEO on How an Introverted Engineer Learned to Lead', *Harvard Business Review*, vol. 94, no. 5, pp. 35–38.

Kirton, MJ, 2011, *Adaption-Innovation in the Context of Diversity and Change*. London: Routledge.

Menold, JM, Jablokow, KW, Purzer, S, Ferguson, DM and Ohland, MW, 2015, 'Using an Instrument Blueprint to Support the Rigorous Development of New Surveys and Assessments in Engineering Education', *ASEE 2015 Annual Conference & Exposition*, Seattle.

Mimaroglu, A, 2016, 'Five Habits that Made Elon Musk an Innovator', *Entrepreneur*. Available at https://wwwentrepreneurcom/article/274417 [Accessed 25 Aug. 2017].

Mumford, MD and Licuanan, B, 2004, 'Leading for Innovation: Conclusions, Issues, and Directions', *Leadership Quarterly*, vol. 15, pp. 163–171.

Paulsen, N, Maldonado, D, Callan, VJ and Ayoko, O, 2009, 'Charismatic Leadership, Change and Innovation in an R&D Organization', *Journal of Organizational Change Management*, vol. 22, no. 5, pp. 511–523.

Paulsen, N, Callan, VJ, Ayoko, O and Saunders, D, 2013, 'Transformational Leadership and Innovation in an R&D Organization Experiencing Major Change', *Journal of Organizational Change Management*, vol. 26, no. 3, pp. 595–610.

Rosen, MA, Bedwell, WL, Wildman, JL, Fritzsche, BA, Salas, E and Burke, CS, 2011, 'Managing Adaptive Performance in Teams: Guiding Principles and Behavioral Markers for Measurement', *Human Resource Management Review*, vol. 21, no. 2, pp. 107–122.

Soken, NH and Kim, BB, 2014, 'What Kills Innovation? Your Role as a Leader in Supporting an Innovative Culture', *Industrial and Commercial Training*, vol. 46, no. 1, pp. 7–15.

Spencer, LM, and Spencer, SM, 1993, *Competence at Work: Models for Superior Performance*. New York: John Wiley & Sons.

Teece, D, 2009, *Managing Intellectual Capital: Organizational, Strategic and Policy Dimensions*. New York: Oxford University Press.

Trott, P, 1998, *Innovation Management and New Product Development*. Upper Saddle River, NJ: Financial Times Pitman Publishing.

Vicere, AA, 1992, 'The Strategic Leadership Imperative for Executive Development', *Human Resource Planning*, vol. 75, no. 1, pp. 15–31.

Vincent, L, 2005, 'Innovation Midwives: Sustaining Innovation Streams in Established Companies', *Research-Technology Management*, vol. 48, no. 1, pp. 41–49.

West, MA, Borrill, CS, Dawson, JF, Brodbeck, F, Shapiro, D and Haward, B, 2003, 'Leadership Clarity and Team Innovation in Health Care', *Leadership Quarterly*, vol. 14, pp. 393–410.

3 Innovation leaders and followership

Patricia Macko and Wesley E. Donahue

The fundamental premise of this chapter is that, in order for innovation leaders to lead teams and achieve successful outcomes, they must understand the concepts of followership and team dynamics. This chapter will define followership, identify the different types of followers, and identify the characteristics that make a successful follower. Likewise, it will define the innovation leader–follower dyad, explore theories related to the innovation leader–follower dyad, and examine innovation leader–follower communication perspectives. Readers also will learn the importance of developing an appreciation and understanding of diversity among innovation leaders and their followers.

Description

While much emphasis has been put on leadership attributes when explaining the roles and characteristics of group or team dynamics, another aspect is often overlooked. This unique aspect is followership. Followership refers to a role held by certain individuals in a group or team environment. Followership is often referred to as the reciprocal social process of leadership (Riggio, 2008). The study of followership involves the examination of the nature and impact of followers and following in the leadership process. The leadership process is a term used to describe leadership as a dynamic system involving leaders and followers interacting simultaneously.

Research foundations

Followers play a powerful role in the successes or failures of organizations, groups and teams. Riggio (2008) states that effective followers are individuals who are enthusiastic, intelligent, ambitious, and self-reliant. Team projects allow both innovation leaders and followers to reproduce their existing norms and values through daily interaction thereby legitimizing their innovation leader–follower relationships. As a form of people management, innovation leaders can use active coaching techniques to ensure followers cultivate teamwork and strong communication. Innovation leaders must also give followers accurate and timely feedback so that they feel valued and show followers that their contribution to the team and to the organization is recognized.

Kelley (1992) summarized behavioral characteristics of four types of followers: alienated, conformist, passive, and exemplary. Alienated followers are mavericks who have a healthy skepticism of the organization. They are capable, but cynical. Conformist followers are the yes people of the organizations. They are very active at doing the organization's work and will actively follow orders. Passive followers rely on leaders to do the thinking for them. They also require constant direction. Exemplary followers are independent, innovative, and willing to question leadership. Kelley (1992) views exemplary followers as critical to organizational success. Exemplary followers know how to work well with other team members and present themselves consistently to all who come into contact with them.

Kelley (1988) described four main qualities of followers. These qualities are: self-management, commitment, competence, and courage. Self-management refers to the ability of group or team members to think critically, control their own actions and to work independently. Commitment refers to the group or team member's ability to be committed to the goal, vision, or cause of the group or team. Competence refers to skills and aptitudes the group or team members hold which are necessary to complete the goals or tasks assigned to the team. Courage refers to the ability of team members to hold steadfast to their beliefs and uphold ethical standards even when faced with dishonest or corrupt leaders. Kelly (1988) also defined two underlying behavioral dimensions for followers. The first behavioral dimension looks at whether or not the team member as an independent, critical thinker. The second dimension refers to whether the team member is active or passive.

There are three leadership theories (see Figure 3.1) that focus on developing the innovation leader–follower dyad including Path-Goal theory, Leader Member Exchange theory, and Diffusion of Innovations theory.

According to House (1975), Path-Goal theory identifies a leader's effectiveness by evaluating a leader's impact on employee motivation, their ability to perform effectively, and their ability to increase employee satisfaction. The major concept of Path-Goal theory is that a leader influences the subordinates' perceptions of their work goals, personal goals, and paths to goal attainment. Innovation leaders, like a trail guide, lead their followers along the path to the goal. The theory suggests that a leader's behavior is motivating or satisfying to the degree that the behavior increases subordinate goal attainment and clarifies the paths to these goals. The first proposition of Path-Goal theory is that leader behavior is acceptable and satisfying to subordinates to the extent that the subordinates see such behavior as either an immediate source of satisfaction or as instrumental to future satisfaction. The second proposition of this theory is that the leader's behavior will be motivational (House, 1975). These motivational behaviors are measured to the extent that (a) such behaviors make the satisfaction of subordinates' needs contingent on effective performance by complementing the environment of

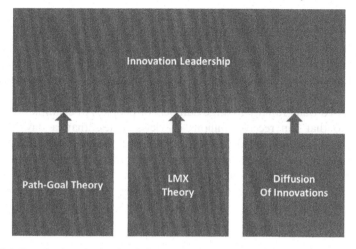

Figure 3.1 Developing the leader–follower dyad with innovation leadership

subordinates and (b) by providing the coaching, guidance, support and rewards necessary for effective performance (House, 1975). These two propositions suggest that the leader's strategic functions are to enhance subordinates' motivation to perform, satisfaction with the job, and acceptance of the leader.

The second theory associated with followership is the Leader Member Exchange (LMX) theory. The major concept of LMX theory is that within work units or teams, different types of relationships develop between leaders and followers (Clarke, 2017). These relationships are depicted by the physical and mental effort, material resources, information, and emotional support exchanged between the leader and follower (Zhichao, 2012). LMX theory is a development-focused theory of leadership and employee development is a key source follower motivation. LMX theory is grounded in role theory. Role theory suggests that organizational or team members accomplish their work through roles or sets of behaviors expected of the team members in their positional roles on the team (Broderick, 1998). Role definition tends to occur when team members are assimilated into new positions on the team and involves the leaders having a vested interest in the performance of that team member. An innovation leader can have a significant impact on the role assignment process because the leader has the authority to negotiate roles using formal methods. Thus, when combined with Path-Goal theory, innovation leaders lead followers along the path to the goal and develop them using LMX theory along the way.

The third theory associated with innovation leader–follower dyad is Diffusion of Innovations theory (DOI). This theory explains how an innovation is communicated through certain channels over time and among members of a social system and is based on many different attributes such as diffusion networks, individual influence, and innovation attributes (Rogers, 2003; Wejnert, 2002). To understand DOI, it is important to use socio-technical systems theory, which explains how people interact with technology in a social system, as a foundation (Hermann, 2007). When an innovation is shared with others, the new idea diffuses among people as they communicate the idea within their social and professional networks. This can happen in live interpersonal interactions and through the use of technology. Many modern communication and social and professional networking platforms allow innovations to be diffused quite rapidly to large numbers of people. An example would be a viral video that can receive millions of views in less than a day. Once the innovation is communicated, it is up to the decision-maker to decide if the innovation is useful. Thus, both the innovation leader and followers play a critical role in deciding if an innovation is successful. The CREATE Model provides a set of steps by which the innovation can be readied for diffusion. Many of the competencies discussed earlier in this book play an important role in how the innovation is developed in the innovation leader–follower dyad.

Application and implementation strategies

A more democratic leadership style may work best when working in a leader–follower dyad (Gastil, 1994). Innovation leaders who possess a democratic leadership style involve followers in setting team guidelines for all to follow, involve followers in setting goals, engage in two-way open communication, facilitate discussion with and amongst followers, solicit input when setting policy and procedures, mediate conflict for team gain, and provide consistent and frequent feedback to followers. Followers bring their individual/internal aspects of their personal internal reality to the team environment. Their internal reality includes attributes such as personal values, attitude, intention and meanings, as well as various experiences. Followers reflect on the 'I' in the team environment as specific relationships. The 'I' is articulated by expressing their intra-personal characteristics such as views, feelings, and intuitions. Innovation leaders must understand that followers differ from one another in many ways. Innovation leaders must find ways to allow each follower to safely bring their own personal attributes to the team environment. This interaction makes up the internal aspects of the innovation leader–follower dyad.

The innovation leader–follower dyad is also made up of an individual's external aspects such as individual knowledge, skills, accountabilities and performance levels. This part of the leader–follower dyad treats followers as catalysts having external aspects which can be measured and defined. Leaders must know how to identify knowledge, competencies and actions of followers in order to achieve the strategic goals of the organization. Leaders must also reinforce desired behaviors of followers such as attendance, following team guidelines, and the ability to bring substantial ideas to innovative team environments (Karaköse, 2011).

In order for both innovation leaders and followers to have successful communication interactions, they must both share critical interpersonal skills with team members (Mencl, 2016). Innovation leaders and followers must be able to engage in the following interpersonal skills.

- Focus on feelings, emotions and attitudes as they relate to personal needs
- Hold open communication at all times
- Communicate through oral and written correspondence
- Actively listen to leader and other team members
- Make requests for assistance and help when needed

It is important for innovation leaders and followers to build a self-awareness of their interpersonal and social styles. By building this self-awareness, leaders and followers create synergy for the team by learning how to communicate in an effective manner. The concept of synergy will be explored in a later chapter of this book.

When leaders and followers understand each other's social style and individual traits, they have the ability to communicate, listen, react, collaborate, and negotiate in an efficient and effective manner for the good of the entire team. Emotional intelligence (EI), sometimes referred to as emotional quotient (EQ), is the capacity for individuals to recognize their own and other people's emotions (Kunnanatt, 2008). The more team members understand about their EI or EQ, the more they can respond the emotional needs of other team members. This understanding helps to guide thinking and leads team members to use appropriate behaviors that will lead to successful team outcomes. Innovation leaders must be aware of the diversity of their followers and how to manage diversity within the team environment. How can innovation leaders do this? First, they need to focus on treating every follower fairly, ethically, and respectfully. Second, leaders need to establish relationships of trust with their followers (Torres, 2012). There are several ways innovation leaders can establish relationships of trust with followers and these are listed below.

- Help followers develop team interaction guidelines.
- Understand how each follower uniquely contributes to the team and recognize their contributions.
- Encourage followers to learn about and respect each other's potentially differing perspectives.
- Show followers that you value their unique individual characteristics and views.
- Assure that you as the leader and all followers treat each other professionally and respectfully at all times.
- Assist followers to build a common focus on the goals of the team.

If a follower does not trust his/her leader, their team will not be able to converse on issues of real significance. Therefore, building trust between innovation leaders and followers is a necessary foundational activity in innovation leadership.

Discussion

Creating and diffusing an innovation requires not only a focus on leadership, but also on followership. Followership is the capacity of individuals to actively follow leaders of innovation initiatives. In order to maximize innovation effectiveness, it is advantageous to have different types of followers as part of initiatives. Researchers have characterized followers in a number of different ways. One way to characterize them is by their behavioral characteristics such as: alienated, conformists, passive, and exemplary. The more innovation leaders increase the knowledge of themselves to and others, the greater their potential for building effective relationships and inspiring innovation (Mencl, 2016).

No matter what follower characteristics are displayed, leaders must recognize that their job is to engage their followers. This requires that leaders create a democratic environment that provides open and honest communication so that followers feel valued and that their contributions to the team and the organization are valued (Gastil, 1994). An effective leader of an innovative organization is inspiring. They make people feel motivated, valued, and excited to innovate on behalf of their organization. Leaders must also be flexible and recognize the value and importance of team diversity and encouraging multiple perspectives. When leaders make their ideas, reasoning, and thinking apparent to others, they build trust over time. As a result, others then become more willing to give them the benefit of the doubt during times when the leader cannot share information.

A leader that values innovation uses trust effectively. A good leader knows that trust goes both ways; you must trust employees to do their jobs well and support the organizational vision and they must be able to trust you to support them, encourage them, and have their back if things go awry (Torres, 2012). Perhaps nothing is more important to the innovation leader–follower relationship than trust. Innovation leaders have a vested interest in helping followers maximize their contributions. They also have a vested interest in providing communication channels for followers to communicate their thoughts and feelings and to inspire others to innovate and to think of better ways to do things.

Summary

This chapter explored the concept of followership and how innovation leaders can be aware of the specific needs of their followers in the innovation leader–follower dyad. The definition, types, and characteristics of followers was explored. Three different theories that are critical to understanding the innovation leader–follower dyad were discussed including Path-Goal theory, Leader Member Exchange theory, and Diffusion of Innovations theory. The chapter continued with a review of different perspectives on leader–follower communication. The chapter concluded with a discussion of how these theories can be applied in organizations.

References

Broderick, AJ, 1998, 'Role Theory, Role Management and Service Performance', *The Journal of Services Marketing*, vol. 12, no. 5, pp. 348–361.

Clarke, N, and Mahadi, N, 2017, 'Differences between Follower and Dyadic Measures of LMX as Mediators of Emotional Intelligence and Employee Performance, Well-being, and Turnover Intention', *European Journal of Work and Organizational Psychology*, vol. 26, no. 3, pp. 373–384.

Gastil, J, 1994, 'A Definition and Illustration of Democratic Leadership', *Human Relations*, vol. 47, no. 8, p. 953.

Hermann, T, Loser, K, and Jahnke, I, 2007, 'Sociotechnical Walkthrough: A Means for Knowledge Integration', *The Learning Organization*, vol. 14, no. 5, pp. 450–464.

House, RJ, and Mitchell, TR, 1975, *Path-goal Theory of Leadership*. Washington University Department of Psychology, Seattle.

Karaköse, T, and Demir, C, 2011, 'Cross-cultural Differentiation and Diversity Management', *International Journal of Business and Commerce*, vol. 1, no. 4, pp. 56–63.

Kelley, RE, 1988 'In Praise of Followers', *Harvard Business Review*, vol. 66, pp. 142–148.

Kelley, R, 1992, *The Power of Followership*. Doubleday, New York.

Kunnanatt, JT, 2008, 'Emotional Intelligence: Theory and Description', *Career Development International*, vol. 13, no. 7, pp. 614–629.

Mencl, J, Wefald, AJ, and van Ittersum, KW, 2016, 'Transformational Leader Attributes: Interpersonal Skills, Engagement, and Well-being', *Leadership & Organization Development Journal*, vol. 37, no. 5, pp. 635–657.

Riggio, RE, Chaleff, I, and Blumen-Lipman, J, 2008, *The Art of Followership: How Great Followers Create Great Leaders and Organizations*, Jossey-Bass, San Francisco.

Rogers, EM, 2003, *Diffusion of Innovations*, Free Press, New York.

Torres, A, and Bligh, M, 2012, 'How far can I Trust You? the Impact of Distance and Cultural Values on Leaders' Trustworthiness', *Journal of Leadership, Accountability and Ethics*, vol. 9, no. 2, pp. 23–38.

Wejnert, B, 2002. 'Integrating Models of Diffusion on Innovations: A Conceptual Framework', *Annual Review of Sociology*, vol. 28, no. 1, pp. 297–326.

Zhichao, C, and Cui, L, 2012, 'Impact of Mean LMX on Team Innovation: An Empirical Study of the Mediating Effect of Team Cooperation and the Moderating Effect of LMX Differentiation in China', *African Journal of Business Management*, vol. 6, no. 35, pp. 9833–9840.

4   Synergies in innovation network teams

Frank Theodore Koe

This chapter will examine synergy in innovation network teams and explore methods that can enhance corporate value and growth. An innovation network team is a cross-functional group that is tasked to create innovations. An innovation network team may be comprised of members from different departments or organizations. An example of an innovation network team in an organization is a new product team. An example of an inter-organizational innovation network team is an industry coalition. Research on innovation explores the role of networks of diverse individuals and organizations (Fischer, 2006). The strong desire for established and start-up organizations to stay ahead of their competition demands that solutions are found to quickly solve complex problems. This implies that team members with appropriate and diverse skill sets interact to create synergy based not only on business practices, but also on a mutual desire to solve problems. In order to understand the implications of creating teams with positive synergy, it is useful to examine some historical foundations of synergy. This backdrop will set the basis for a discussion on how the culture of a company can provide innovation leadership and design innovation network teams that promote, fuel, and foster creativity.

As discussed earlier in the book, diverse people who bring differing mindsets to a group should be carefully managed so they can cooperatively build solutions in an environment of trust. Individually, one person who does not match the energy, purpose, desire, and passion of the group can be a detriment. Similarly, one member of the team cannot be a predictor of positive outcomes. It is the combined mix of the right individuals where synergy is formed that can result in innovative solutions to challenging problems. Innovation leaders need to understand the psychological aspects of synergy for team composition and to more fully understand their role.

Description

To understand synergy, it may be useful to begin with a definition. Synergy originated from the Greek word '*sunergos*' meaning 'working together.' One way of understanding synergy is to consider the composition of water. Water, or H_2O, is composed of the merger of oxygen and hydrogen. Each element is independent of the another, but when correctly combined atomically, a new substance is formed. The human body provides a good example to understanding synergy. To know how a particular bodily function works, it is necessary to study individual systems and subsystems.

Synergy in the workplace is a complex concept that goes beyond placing random individuals in teams and assigning them a task to complete. Innovation leaders should carefully understand the capabilities of individuals and what they can contribute. If a goal is to climb over a ten-foot high wall, one person alone may not be able to achieve the task. But, two well-coordinated individuals can accomplish the task by one person standing on the shoulders of the other. The key is that they need to work together, be motivated to climb to the top of the wall, and be physically capable. In business, firms merge to create opportunity and increased value that one company alone could not achieve. But, not all attempts to create synergy are successful and can actually detract from a set of goals. For example, if a global organization wishes to merge or develop synergy with a foreign entity and does not consider its culture, the result could be wasted time, energy, and money. Forced intervention by company executives who choose to dominate another company or culture will not ensure synergy. Synergy, therefore, must be carefully managed.

When exploring synergy, innovation, and innovation leadership, it is essential for one to be comfortable in acknowledging what one does not know. Once this becomes internalized and accepted, new learning can be realized and innovations can be developed in innovation network teams. It is important for an innovation leader to ask challenging questions without fear of judgement. In corporate environments, emphasis is commonly placed on individual problem-solving. Synergy in a corporate structure acknowledges what people know and do not know and how they work together to fill in the knowledge gaps in a cooperative, supportive way. If synergy is encouraged, everyone is acknowledged for having worth and every employee can contribute fearlessly. Respect for the individual using a philosophy of personalism is paramount.

Research foundations

Research and literature about synergy and its connection to innovation network teams has origins in sociology, management theory, organizational behavior, psychology, group and intergroup relations, network theory and modeling, and entrepreneurship and intrapreneurship. Early references to synergy, however, are related to religion. As time progressed, literature on synergy was developed in the field of social psychology by the likes of Mazel (1896). His thesis was that society was not developed by the elite members solely, but also by the masses collectively working together to build social systems that benefited everyone. Ward (1918) spoke of social synergy as a struggle between two social political movements that, when combined over time, formed a constructive social order. Synergy also has roots in systems theory as related to biology, physiology, and medicine particularly with regard to how drugs interact with each other. In Dunglison's (1853) book *Medical Lexicon*, the connectedness between different organs and living systems is made clear. Synergy in nature, as in an innovative corporate environment, relies on individual elements, or people, working cooperatively in an effort to achieve effects that are not otherwise possible (Corning, 2003). Also in nature, the idea of symbiosis is relevant where there is a biological linkage between two different species each depending on one another, creating a system of mutual dependency (de Bary, 1887).

One of the earliest references in the United States of applying the principles of synergy comes from Benjamin Franklin. In Franklin's (1793) auto-biography, *The Private Life of the late Benjamin Franklin*, he described founding a group of individuals collectively known as Junto in 1727. Junto, loosely translated, means to join. Harnessing his natural desire for building up his own personal social capital, Franklin populated Junto with people of varying backgrounds and professions for the purpose of learning and improving themselves. The meetings were reported to be positive and cordial and centered on questions that Franklin developed. Present-day Junto orga-nizations exist such as The Junto Institute for Entrepreneurial Leadership in Chicago or CoIN, a web social entity that promotes open collaboration within and outside organizations. These, along with industry coalitions, pro-fessional organizations, and cross-functional teams are great examples of innovation network teams. Today, globalization coupled with multiple forms of communication has provided a way for teams to rapidly organize in a see-mingly organic way, as in biology, for the purpose of inventing solutions free from the interference of traditional managers.

Considerable literature exists on synergy that relates to psychology and personality theory. To develop synergy, one should focus on achieving a goal with a team altruistically. In our highly competitive, well educated, and fast-paced society, it is common to find employees with aggressive ambition working to move up the corporate ladder by harming people who get in their way. To have synergy, individuals should possess a calling where one believes that what they do for work contributes to a higher good (Wrzesniewski, 2003). This notion has a basis in Goldstein's (1939) work on self-actualized behavior that states that an individual should strive to be the best they can be. Building on Goldstein's (1939) work, Maslow (1943) developed the hierarchy of needs and in doing so described synergy as that which is beneficial for an individual is beneficial for everyone. From this position, Maslow (1943) moved self-actualization into the realm of team decision-making and business synergy.

Innovation leaders should reflect on work as a source of becoming self-actualized. Demonstrating personality traits such as calmness, confidence, and competency can be motivating to team members. Likewise, research has indicated that extrinsic rewards are not always the best source of workplace motivation. Instead, intrinsic rewards, such as making a difference based on the meaningfulness of what one accomplishes, can carry more weight (Ariely, 2008). Likewise, workplace compensation is often based upon responsibility, so those focusing on intrinsic rewards such as professional development to gain more workplace responsibility may achieve additional extrinsic rewards in the long-term with high performance and opportunity for promotion. People want to contribute, and in doing so, gain personal satisfaction that they can contribute to the common good. Work can be a virtue in itself.

An innovation leader is outgoing, social, and looks to the positive attributes of people while challenging himself or herself to become self-actualized. These behavioral traits set up an environment for learning and problem solving using a non-intervening management approach as defined by Maslow (1943). Synergy, therefore, begins with freeing up restraints about how one may be judged, and working to demonstrate a mutual respect for team members and the talents they possess for solving problems in a cooperative and humanistic setting. Once the stage is set for collective performance, the challenge of achieving positive synergy is well worth the effort. Studies in self-actualization of small business owners who are merchandising-oriented (Lessner, 1974) have been found to be more actualized than craft-oriented entrepreneurs. The networking activities involved in sales professions are social and therefore connecting. Likewise, the role of striving for self-actualization results in a content and productive worker that utilizes all aspects of their capabilities in a positive environment (Shostrom, 1987). Difficulties can arise, however, when attempting to correlate self-actualized workers and organizational performance (Dorer, 2006). Innovation leaders should understand the composition of personalities in an innovation network team. Likewise, team members should learn about themselves. Helping people become their honest self in the workplace by establishing a new working environment centered on effective communication can help to develop the synergy of the innovation network team.

Personality tests such as Meyers-Briggs Type Indicator (MBTI) or other similar tests can be useful tools to help team members understand each other's personalities. The MBTI examines self-understanding and how to understand others based on archetypes developed by Jung (1971) using personality traits such as sensation, intuition, feeling, and thinking. The MBTI should be administered by a trained professional. However, there are many other similar tests that can be freely used based on Jung's (1971) work for self-assessment. Although any personality assessment test can be criticized for producing results that may not be accurate or relevant, they can be helpful as a point of discussion on the synergy of a team. Thus, synergy is about learning characteristics of people that may not be self-evident.

Synergy between organizations is an outgrowth of well-defined intra-organizational structures. As businesses strive to improve their supply chain, culture, technology, and people must connect in a synchronized way to deliver on commitments. Effort needs to be placed on best practices to keep products flowing. Because businesses are typically organized into functional units, the units must communicate and coordinate efforts. Best practices centered around adaptation, effort incentives, and information can achieve harmony and a degree of synergy (Dessein, 2010). Companies in the process of a merger or acquisition experience more synergy than a single company that is merely growing larger. In order for corporate synergy to work well, careful consideration should be given to whether or not customers can or will continue to do business with the new entity. Likewise, financial conditions should be considered. However, it is the personal interactions that business leaders have with their business partners that can indicate if a merger or acquisition will be successful.

Application and implication strategies

Developing synergy in a team that is driven by the differences of its members (Covey, 2004) can be challenging in an established company in contrast to a start-up where familiarity among team members may have developed organically. Regardless of how or where the team assembled, the reality is that for innovation to occur, it is important for innovation leaders to understand the synergy of their innovation network team. When leading creative people, three elements should be considered: head, heart, and hand. Head is what people know. Do those being considered for team membership have knowledge that is appropriate for and complimentary to their fellow team members? Heart is the passion and spirit one should possess to be energized about the task at hand and the ability to persist in light of setbacks. Hand means to be personally and positively motivated and committed to do what needs to be done. The concepts of head, heart, and hand should be part of the team's long-term strategy. Teams are effective when the members are skilled and emotionally invested.

In the context of organizational behavior and corporate strategy, it is essential for a company and, more specifically, the innovation leader to create a culture of openness, support, and positive communication. Innovation leaders and team members need to be open to possibilities from diverse group members and strive to attract and retain individuals using talent management strategies. Activities that bring employees together help to create and maintain team synergy. Innovation leaders should demonstrate caring behaviors toward their employees and suggest team building activities to build synergy. Group picnics or other kinds of outings help bring employees closer. At Optima Group USA located on the North Shore of Chicago, senior management purchased scooters so employees can travel from the company to scenic Lake Michigan. At Optima, employees are part of the decision-making process. The more successful the team becomes, the more successful individual team members are (Archer, 2006).

One of the most influential and powerful notions that an organization can develop in its employees is a belief in and the ownership of the mission, values, culture, and goals. Understanding and freely agreeing with a company's value proposition is also important. This means that a company's product or service should create value for the customer. It gives the customer a reason for purchasing the product or service because the organization is delivering the specific benefits the customer is seeking. Thus, customer satisfaction is the source of sustainable value creation. From a marketing and sales perspective, the emphasis is less on the Old Four Ps: Product, Price, Promotion, and Placement, where the focus was on market dominance. Today, the emphasis is instead on the New Four Ps: Purpose, People, Personal, and Perception, where the key question is, does your product offering matter? If employees care and genuinely believe in the value of their work and fully embrace why they are doing it, others will believe so too and buy into the company's culture and what they are offering. One example of this is the rise of the iPhone. Early adopters continue to stand in line for hours to be among the first to own the latest phone even though other companies have developed similar technologies and products.

There are many similarities between the synergies that are supported within individual corporate teams and intra-organizational units. Considering intra-organizational synergy, there are practical guidelines summarized by Hansen (2009).

- Expand the company outward to build and enhance social capital with unfamiliar individuals.
- Choose diversity of talent over hiring people with similar traits.
- Look for people who have longevity with the firm so as to more easily connect with others.
- Build on reciprocity to share and exchange information to build trust.

The focus of each guideline remains the same: listen and strive to satisfy customer wants and needs by knowing what they wish to buy and use technology to target them. Finally, it is also critical to become familiar with Efficient Consumer Response (ECR) as a way of working in harmony with suppliers.

Discussion

Everyone has value. The key for developing synergy in an innovation network team is shifting management thinking from command and control to coordinate and cultivate. In this environment, individuals are more empowered and less encumbered by the presence of varying management levels and bureaucracy. Another benefit of this management approach is improved communication between employees and other group members. A flat organizational structure can contribute to some confusion due to the lack of a controlling hierarchical structure, but these issues are mitigated by placing importance on the work environment, culture, and mission of a company. Flat organizational structures are often evident in universities, internet-based firms, and even Lockheed Martin's Skunkworks. Often, flat organizational structures allow for stronger mentoring relationships among employees and encourage higher performance because this type of environment encourages self-starters to thrive. However, larger organizations typically do have hierarchical structures that often inhibit the free flow of information. In such an organizational structure, administrators usually confine their interactions to other administrators rarely taking into consideration what line employees think. In such a system, vital links can be missed creating a disassociation from the customer that can have negative effects on corporate profit.

Organizations with flat hierarchies have a shorter chain of command, are more cost effective, promote faster decision-making, invite synergy, but are typically smaller in size. Companies that are organized in small teams with strong synergy have a better chance to be in touch with customers and therefore, remain responsive to their needs. The prerequisites for developing group synergy in a flat organization include: interacting, appreciative understanding, integrating, and implementing (Conner, 2011). This approach also casts a favorable light on external partners and investors who learn that the objectives of a firm are larger than any one person. In a horizontal or flat organization, the notion of ambition is viewed differently than in a hierarchical organization. Likewise, managing growth within a flat organization can be a challenge. The challenges of maintaining the core principals and energy of a start-up require effort, but can be maintained through communication and transparency and having employees fully invested in the company.

Summary

Sourcing from biology, psychology, and organizational management, the notion of synergy has permeated start-ups and larger companies alike. With more companies looking for innovation leaders to support growth in small to medium-sized enterprises, there has been a rise in the number of entrepreneurial programs offered by US colleges and universities. Companies are learning that returning to basics where the customer is central to sustained growth is simply good for business. If corporations pay close attention to issues of employee retention, they may notice that oftentimes key people leave a firm because they want more autonomy and in doing so go on to develop competitive businesses. Many companies have spent considerable sums to acquire a firm that they could have started with their own employees. The challenge for existing companies is to look to their culture to see if they are standing still or moving ahead. Do they have the capacity for change? The speed that business must adapt and the speed with which customers purchase product, particularly via the internet, is astounding. Developing a plan to incorporate synergy into a firm can serve to build a corporate community that is responsive, interconnected, humane, and sustainable.

References

Archer, A and Walczyk, D, 2006, 'Driving creativity and innovation through culture in corporate creativity', *Design Management Review*, Summer.

Ariely, D, 2008, *Predictable irrational: the hidden forces that sharpen decisions*, Harper Collins, New York.

Conner, D, 2011, 'Four ways communication can build synergy in work teams'. Blogpost on Managing at the speed of change.

Corning, P, 2003, *Nature's magic: synergies in evolution and fate of humankind*, Cambridge University Press, London.

Covey, SR, 2004, *The seven habits of highly effective people*, Free Press, New York.

De Bary, A, 1887, *Lectures on bacteria*. Second improved edition, University Press, London.

Dessein, W and Garicano, R, 2010, 'Organizing for synergies', *American Economic Journal: Microeconomics*, vol. 2, pp 77–114.

Dorer, HL and Mahoney, JM, 2006, 'Self-actualization in the corporate hierarchy', *North American Journal of Psychology*, vol. 8, no. 2, pp. 321–328.

Dunglison, R, 1853, *Medical lexicon: a dictionary of medical science*, Blanchard & Lea, Philadelphia.

Fischer, MM, 2006, *Innovation, networks, and knowledge spillovers, selected essays*, Springer, Berlin.

Franklin, B, 1793, *The private life of the late Benjamin Franklin*, L.L.D., London.

Goldstein, K, 1939, *The organism: a holistic approach to biology derived from pathological data in man*, Zone Books, New York.

Hansen, MT, 2009, *Collaboration: how leaders avoid the traps, create unity, and reap big results*, Harvard Business Review, Boston.

Jung, CG, 1971, *Psychology types: collected works of C G Yung*, Princeton University Press, Princeton, NJ.

Lessner, M and Knapp, R, 1974, 'Self-actualization and entrepreneurial orientation among small business owners: a validation study of the POI', *Educational and Psychological Management*, vol. 34, no. 2, pp. 455–460.

Maslow, A, 1943, 'A theory of human motivation', *Psychological Review*, vol. 50, no. 4, pp. 370–396.

Maslow, A, 1965, *Eupsychian Management*, R.D. Irwin, London.

Mazel, H, 1896, *La synergie sociale*, Paris, France.

Shostrom, EL, 1987, *Personal orientation inventory manual*, Edits Publishers, San Diego, CA.

Ward, FL, 1918, *Vol. VI, Glimpses of the cosmos (1897–1912)*, G.P. Putman & Sons, New York.

Wrzesniewski, A, 2003, 'Finding positive meaning in work'. In Cameron, K, Dutton, J and Quinn, R, eds., *Positive organizational scholarship: foundations of a new discipline*, Berrett-Kohler, Oakland, CA.

5 Building a culture of continuous innovation

Jong Gyu Park and Wesley E. Donahue

It is crucial for organizations to build and maintain a culture of continuous innovation to be successful. Organizational culture is a set of values, beliefs, and ways of thinking shared by members of the organization (Schein, 2010). According to Gliddon (2006), "as innovations become more radical, management of organizational culture is key" (p. 20). Innovation leaders are able to foster and promote organizational cultures that spark creativity and risk-taking, motivate and reward employees to think out of the box, and channel ideas to increase stakeholder value (Ahmed, 1998). However, these characteristics are not easily replicated by those organizations most in need of developing a culture of continuous innovation. In this chapter, you will gain an understanding of how innovation leaders assess, clarify, and communicate an organization's culture and values; how they design and implement a new organizational culture; and how they build new roles and responsibilities to support innovation.

Description

Innovation creates a mindset to envision, shape, and attack the future (Davila, Epstein, and Shelton, 2012). Although much has been written about innovation, it often remains an organizational initiative shrouded with uncertainty. Many organizational leaders do not know where to begin, how to unleash the creative potential of their employees, or how to equip leaders with the right competencies to lead innovation. In other words, many understand the 'why' of innovation but are still unclear about the 'what' and 'how'. Building a culture of continuous innovation can help to address the 'what' and the 'how' of innovation. In this chapter, we will answer for the three key questions:

- What is organizational culture and why is it important?
- What is a culture of continuous innovation?
- How do we build a culture of continuous innovation?

Likewise, we will explore the role of the innovation leadership in building a culture of continuous innovation because one of the biggest influences on innovation is an organization's culture.

Research foundations

Organizational culture is reflected in the way that people relate to each other, to the organization, and the organization's environment (Ahmed, 1998; Lau and Ngo, 2004). An organization's culture responds to the organizational environment, structures day-to-day work assignments, and rewards the talents of its people. Besides performance, an organization's culture uniquely distinguishes an organization from other organizations. Employees internalize values, beliefs, norms, and behaviors to fit into the culture of the organization, do their work, and interact with each other professionally. An organization's culture develops over time and is subject to a variety of positive and negative influences. The vision of a founder who has since left the organization, conditions that are not typical or expected to repeat, and practices that were coincident with, but not actually responsible for, the organization's success are examples of such influences. Thus, as an organization grows and matures, the culture may encourage and reward practices and policies that are not appropriate for or counter-productive to the needs of a changing organization, especially for a culture of continuous innovation.

Changes in the market, customer needs and preferences, technology, or the availability of resources all point to the need for developing an adaptive culture that can effectively carry an organization through most situations. If there is misalignment between the organization's strategy, its vision for the future, and its current organizational culture, an organization may be less likely to meet its goals. Thus, to be successful, leaders need to develop an organizational culture that fits an organization's objectives with its strategy (Butts, 2012). For example, work processes need to be tailored to the types of products or services offered and value-driven human resources practices should be aligned. If organizations pursue and articulate an innovation strategy, the organization needs to have a culture of continuous innovation aligned to its innovation strategy.

In a culture of continuous innovation, there are cultural relationships among creativity, innovation, and implementation in a dynamic cycle (see Figure 5.1) such that: (a) creativity is the wellspring of ideas that feed

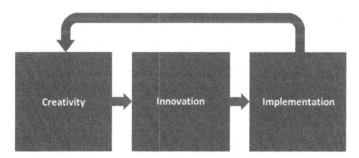

Figure 5.1 Dynamic cycle of creativity, innovation, and implementation

innovation, (b) an innovation happens when creative ideas are transformed into realistic action plans, and (c) implementation fosters additional creativity.

Considering creativity, organizations can establish creativity as a core organizational value and criteria for acquiring and developing talent. In regard to innovation, organizations can communicate the importance of innovations and their quantifiable impact on the organization. An organization can then set measureable innovation goals and allow employees the freedom to choose how they are to be achieved. During implementation, organizations can streamline work processes into project-based activities, review performance and progress toward goals, and provide rewards for achieving goals.

Once the dynamic cycle of creativity, innovation, and implementation in a culture of continuous innovation is initialized, organizations can begin to change their culture. Strong culture has been linked to organizational short-term performance (Denison, 1990; Gordon and DiTomaso, 1992). However, strong cultures do not necessarily create sustainable long-term performance. Therefore, cultural change should be linked to the organization's climate and core strategy. Organizations commonly change to a culture of continuous innovation to develop a strategy of sustainable growth. Although it is sometimes challenging, changing an organization's culture is possible if it is managed in steps (Lewis, 1996). The following is a set of steps organizations can use to develop a culture of continuous innovation. Innovation leaders should help members of organizations answer the questions included in each step.

Step 1. Plan a cultural assessment.

- What does the organization's innovation strategy tell us about the culture?
- Who are the innovation leaders and key stakeholders in the organization?
- What else do we know about the culture? Still need to know?

Step 2. Define the culture of continuous innovation.

- What is the organization's vision/mission and what part does innovation play?
- What do we want people to understand and believe about innovation?
- What are the desired innovation competencies, behaviors, and practices?

Step 3. Audit existing organizational cultures.

- What organizations have a culture of innovation?
- What are their innovation competencies, behaviors, and practices?
- What are current attitudes toward innovation?
- How effective is communication in the organization?

Step 4. Analyze the gaps.

- What are the similarities and differences between the existing cultures and our desired culture?
- How big are the gaps and what is the risk?

Step 5. Plan the transition.

- How can we close the gaps?
- How can we motivate people to change?
- What is the priority and timing of the action plan?
- How will we measure the success of the cultural change?

Application and implementation strategies

Innovation is one way organizations can achieve success by improving processes and creating a workforce that is more productive. However, several recent studies have stated that, if organizations fail to build a culture of innovation and properly address cultural issues, they may fail in pursuing organization-wide innovations (Patel, Kohtamäki, Parida, and Wincent, 2015; Van der Panne, Van Beers, and Kleinknecht, 2003). Therefore, we recommend assessing an organization's culture as part of its innovation strategy. This will provide the organization with quantitative and qualitative knowledge about its culture. This knowledge can be used to compare the organization with other organizations that have successfully developed a culture of innovation. This knowledge can also be used to evaluate and select potential strategies for developing a culture of continuous innovation. Organizations that have started to develop an innovation strategy should consider conducting a cultural assessment after a six-month to one-year period. Organizations should seek to align their organizational culture with their strategy for innovation using an integrated view. This integrated view of organizational culture (see Figure 5.2) provides a comprehensive framework for understanding and assessing an organization's culture.

How does an innovation leader decide if an organization's culture enables or is a barrier to successful innovation? The first step in conducting a cultural

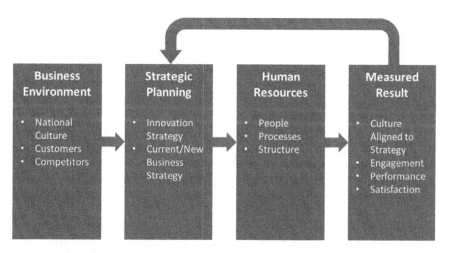

Figure 5.2 Building a culture of continuous innovation

assessment is to articulate the organization's vision and innovation strategy to determine the culturally driven practices and behaviors that will enable them. The next step is an assessment of the current culture and an analysis of the gap between the current and the desired innovation culture. An organizational culture assessment, such as Park and Donohue's *Culture of Continuous Innovation Assessment* can be administered to employees and is an excellent way to assess the current culture and obtain the information needed to conduct the gap analysis. When conducting an organizational culture survey, employees provide quantitative and qualitative information on the way organizational and innovation-focused policies and practices are actually working in an organization. An employee survey also provides information on how employees' view their relationship with the organization. An examination of formal policies may not reveal whether employees believe they are being treated equitably, whether they trust management, or feel engaged in the organization. Because employee perceptions help to drive their work behavior, it is essential to gather this type of information. Employee data is more than employee opinion, it is essential information about the organization that can be used by innovation leaders to plan successful innovations and develop organizational sustainability.

Globalization has connected markets globally and has led to an increase in workplace and organizational activities abroad (Scholte, 2000). Globalization has created a need to understand how business is conducted in many different economic, social, and political environments. When considering the fit between an organization's innovation strategy and its culture, a multinational organization must take into account the differing national values that may place constraints on organizational practices in its operations throughout the world. Globalization effects organizations in two ways. First, organizations need to reflect the culture in which they originate. South Korean employees, for example, in comparison to U.S. employees, tend to emphasize group behavior and performance over individual performance (Rhee, Park and Lee, 2010). Thus, an organizational culture that requires a high degree of teamwork may benefit from South Korean team-building strategies. Second, organizations doing business in countries with different cultures need to adapt their organizational culture to interact productively with businesses based on dissonant cultural values. For example, Company A from the United States believes in taking a fair amount of risk when expanding its business. However, its branch office abroad does business in an environment that does not value financial risks. To expand its business in that country, the branch office may have to borrow money locally, but local banks will not consider the organization a good candidate for a loan because they perceive its behavior to be too risky. Thus, multinational organizations need to adapt their cultures and strategies to be compatible with local organizational practices and national cultural values. Modern trends in globalization may someday lead to a relatively homogeneous global culture that will soften national differences in organizations (Guillen, 2001; Larson, 2002). However, in today's business world, it is essential to pinpoint and resolve existing conflicts between national and organizational culture for successful innovation (Tödtling and Trippl, 2005).

Discussion

The ability to innovate is a critical benchmarking criterion that differentiates high performing companies from the ravaged ones (Hull and Rothenberg, 2008). Innovation can make a drastic difference in an organization's success by reducing time-to-market for new products and services, improving processes, creating cost efficiencies, and fostering a workforce that is better informed, more productive, and finds greater fulfillment in the workplace. Sustainable innovation requires a positive culture. Innovative organizations foster and develop a culture of continuous innovation that encourages employee creativity and motivates them to improve performance. Innovation is more than just the buzzword of the week. Therefore, short-term cultural development programs are ineffective without long-term strategies. Employees become inured and resistant to a one-time flurry of attention and activity followed by business as usual. What is needed is fundamental and lasting change in all aspects of the organization. Thus, it is important to review and update the HR function in areas such as job descriptions, training and development, compensation, benefits, organizational structure, staffing processes, and employee safety and security initiatives.

An organization's HR strategy is influenced by its cultural values. When the HR strategies and practices are not aligned with the organization's overall strategy, productivity and performance can suffer. For example, an organization whose strategy requires continuous innovation, development of new products and teamwork will be more effective if the organization also values and practices knowledge-sharing among teams and employees. Understanding the practices associated with effective HR and the values underlying these practices will help organizations to optimally align their culture with their organizational strategy. In addition, a culture of continuous innovation can attract and retain employees and help to develop their talent.

To build a culture of continuous innovation, innovation leaders should focus on achieving a lasting competitive advantage, developing new roles that support innovation, encouraging high performance, and implementing employee reward systems that measure innovation. Assessing your organization's culture is a great place to start. By measuring the culture's alignment with its strategy, innovation leaders are able to quantify the organization's cultural gaps and create actionable steps. The structured, analytical approach described in this chapter can unleash the creativity of employees and help your organization to develop a culture of continuous innovation.

Summary

This chapter discussed the importance of building a culture of continuous innovation. It explored the relationship between an organizational culture and innovation. It reviewed the dynamic cycle of creativity, innovation, and implementation, and its foundations. In addition, this chapter discussed how to assess, identify, and communicate the organizational culture and its values to support innovation. It reviewed a set of steps organizations can use to develop a culture of continuous innovation. This chapter looked at the role that HR plays when developing a culture of continuous innovation. In this chapter, we answered three key questions:

1   What is an organizational culture, and why is it important? Organizational culture refers to the values and behaviors of an organization. While organizational culture can be informed by an organization's stated mission, vision, and goals, it is also characterized by its performance, values, beliefs, and ways of thinking shared by members of the organization. An organization's culture is generally created by its leaders. How leaders communicate, behave, what actions they model, and what they expect from their employees sets the tone of the organizational culture. Organizational culture is important because it unites an organization's human resources to achieve the organization's goals and objectives.

2   What is a culture of continuous innovation? A culture of continuous innovation is characterized by a dynamic cycle of creativity, innovation, and implementation. Creativity is the wellspring of ideas that feed innovation. An innovation happens when creative ideas are transformed into realistic action plans. Implementation fosters additional creativity. This process subsequently fosters additional creative ideas. Creating a culture of innovation typically starts when innovation leaders establish an innovation strategy.

3   How do we build a culture of continuous innovation? Without innovation, an organization becomes stagnant and change is needed to make it sustainable. Successful organizations often describe success in terms of creating new products or services, streamlining processes, and eliminating waste. However, a culture of continuous innovation is multi-faceted and includes periodic assessment of other factors, such as organizational plans, work systems, communications/decision making, managerial leadership, and training/rewards. Changing or building a culture of continuous innovation that is truly effective and transforming for the organization has at least three components. First, the organization's culture must be understood and deliberately crafted. Second, leaders must understand and embrace innovation. Third, employees must understand and buy-into the culture, realize the organization's goals related to innovation, and feel empowered to be innovative. Building a culture of continuous innovation creates a mindset to envision and shape the future.

References

Ahmed, PK, 1998, 'Culture and climate for innovation', *European Journal of Innovation Management*, vol. 1, no. 1, pp. 30–43.

Butts, JB, 2012, 'Ethics in organizations and leadership', In JB Butts and KL Rich, eds, *Nursing ethics: Across the curriculum and into practice*, 4th edn, pp. 399–427, Jones & Bartlett Learning, Sudbury, MA.

Davila, T, Epstein, M, and Shelton, R, 2012, *Making innovation work: How to manage it, measure it, and profit from it*, Wharton School Publishing, Upper Saddle River, NJ.

Denison, DR, 1990, *Corporate culture and organizational effectiveness*, Wiley, New York.

Gliddon, DG, 2006, 'Forecasting a competency model for innovation leaders using a modified Delphi technique'. PhD. The Pennsylvania State University.

Gordon, GG, and DiTomaso, N, 1992, 'Predicting corporate performance from organizational culture', *Journal of Management Studies*, vol. 29, no. 6, pp. 783–798.

Guillen, MF, 2001, 'Is globalization civilizing, destructive or feeble? A critique of five key debates in the social science literature', *Annual Review of Sociology*, vol. 27, pp. 235–260.

Hull, CE, and Rothenberg, S, 2008, 'Firm performance: The interactions of corporate social performance with innovation and industry differentiation', *Strategic Management Journal*, vol. 29, no. 7, pp. 781–789.

Larson, R, 2002, 'Globalization, societal change, and new technologies: What they mean for the future of adolescence', *Journal of Research on Adolescence*, vol. 12, pp. 1–30.

Lau, CM, and Ngo, HY, 2004, 'The HR system, organizational culture, and product innovation', *International Business Review*, vol. 13, no. 6, pp. 685–703.

Lewis, D, 1996, 'The organizational culture saga – from OD to TQM: A critical review of the literature part 2 – applications', *Leadership & Organization Development Journal*, vol. 17, no. 2, pp. 9–16.

Patel, PC, Kohtamäki, M, Parida, V, and Wincent, J, 2015, 'Entrepreneurial orientation-as-experimentation and firm performance: The enabling role of absorptive capacity', *Strategic Management Journal*, vol. 36, no. 11, pp. 1739–1749.

Rhee, J, Park, T, and Lee, DH, 2010, 'Drivers of innovativeness and performance for innovative SMEs in South Korea: Mediation of learning orientation', *Technovation*, vol. 30, no. 1, pp. 65–75.

Schein, EH, 2010, *Organizational culture and leadership*, 4th edn, Jossey-Bass, San Francisco.

Scholte, JA, 2000, *Globalization: A critical introduction*, Palgrave, Basingstoke, UK.

Tödtling, F, and Trippl, M, 2005, 'One size fits all? Towards a differentiated regional innovation policy approach', *Research Policy*, vol. 34, no. 8, pp. 1203–1219.

Van der Panne, G, Van Beers, C, and Kleinknecht, A, 2003, 'Success and failure of innovation: A literature review' *International Journal of Innovation Management*, vol. 7, no. 3, pp. 309–338.

6 You have the idea, now how do you fund it?

Juliette Kleinmann

So, you have an innovative idea? How do you get your leadership team to get on board to fund it? Innovations require funding and the persuasion of leadership teams to support the initiative. Draper (2015) makes a poignant connection between the business engine and the fuel of funding. Without fuel the engine cannot run and without funding an innovation cannot be realized. Whether your idea is meant for a large scale, small scale or entrepreneur level implementation, the identification of a return on investment (ROI) is necessary to add value.

Often the method to identify funding falls on the innovation leader. Gathering a cost analysis and expense forecasting are critical in obtaining approval for the evolution of the innovation. Additionally, calculating the return on investment is not only empirical, but prudent to establish the value of the innovation. Having a working knowledge of the different aspects or means of potential funding may help to provide your idea with the extra emphasis it needs to be seen as a valuable or necessary project by management or investors. Understanding who your stakeholders are and their role in giving your idea the go ahead is just as important as your idea or funding analysis. These stakeholders are looking not only at the innovation, but also the bottom line financial impact of the innovation.

The stakeholders and scale of the innovation help to recognize and identify what should be included in a financial plan. However, the importance of a financial plan depends on factors beyond the stakeholders and scale. Consideration must also be given to compartmentalization into different levels of expenses. The different levels of expense based on factors such as; ground work (expertise, research), technology costs (both physical, human), testing (both integration, regression), marketing and training. Knowing this pushes the innovator into potential areas of inexperience when trying to identify the elements of cost. The innovator must think beyond the idea itself and determine what, who or how the idea touches cost.

Description

Innovations often require innovative methods to fund them. Lewandowska (2013) raises the point that the complexity of raising funds for an innovation can be risky and sometimes difficult. However, this should not dissuade an innovation leader as there are many ways to present a request for funding. It all depends on the environment of the innovation and the audience it is presented to. Building the ground work to identify the costs associated with the research and implementation provides the innovation leader with a solid footing when approaching leadership teams to fund an innovation. This means the innovation leader needs to understand some common concepts in not only the ability to identify costs, but also in the value the innovation presents for the future.

Finding the starting point begins with finding each cost step that the innovation touches. To find these you have to think about not only the implantation but also development. Since you know the end product you need to know the starting point. Often you must think beyond the innovation and onto more practical needs; these could include:

- The number of programmers needed, their hourly rate and length of time needed.
- The number of project team members needed, their hourly rate and length of time needed.
- The amount of systemic testing needed, and the cost of the testing whether internal or external.
- What materials will need to be tested to implement the idea?
- Are there outside factors such as regression testing or training needs?
- Is the idea a technological advancement, new product, change in procedure/process?
- Are there copyright or patent concerns?

With these questions answered you can be well prepared to determine what the cost of the innovation would most likely be. However, this may take some leg work and partnership with other teams within your business. If you fear you are not qualified to provide such an analysis, invoke your network of colleagues. Utilize your partnerships within your systems, finance and business lines to help in defining each point you will need for your cost benefit analysis.

Building your financial foundation starts with a cost benefit analysis (CBA). A CBA is used to estimate the benefits versus the costs associated with any given project (Weimer, 2011). It applies a monetary valuation to the potential benefit that may present on any given project (Hwang, 2015). One important thing to note is that costs and benefits can occur at different times in a project cycle and therefore fully vetting the innovation is recommended (O'Brien, 2015). There are several factors to consider when doing a CBA. Costs include items such as those listed above; time, payroll, testing, materials, technology, as well as licensing, patents and legal fees (O'Brien, 2015). Benefits can include additional sales, improvements in processes, reduction in risks, efficiency and advantages in competitiveness (O'Brien, 2015). The CBA provides you with a clear idea of what expenses you will need to cover in your presentation to management. Additionally, it also presents you with an opportunity to identify if a capital expense is required.

Understanding capital expense or expenditure is essential when the innovation will require a large investment on the part of the business. Larger businesses have more ability to use a capital expense due to the ability to make a financially sound decision to expend the large amount of funds that are required (Leong, 2014). Capital expenditures carry one major difference from operation expenditures and that is based on the fact that a capital expenditure is based on an asset that expands a benefit beyond a single year (Gitman, 2012). The motivation behind using a capital expenditure to fund an innovation is to expand upon the current business, enhance the business or invest in a new idea. These are long-term expenditures. With long-term expenditures comes risk (Moffett, 2009). For this reason, it is imperative you provide full disclosure when presenting the financial framework of your innovation. A capital expense can be substantiated by presenting a return on the long-term investment.

A return on investment deals with knowing what the profit is on the investment that is made (Bendle, 2016). What benefit will the innovation have in the future and can that benefit be equated to a financial gain? Think of this as a long-term goal. You are making a financial assessment of the value that will be gained if the idea comes to fruition (Arney, 2017). While the innovation may cost in the first year or even the longer term, what will the idea provide in terms of profit in the long run. Identifying the progress of the profit line is important to your stakeholders. Initially you may have costs associated with training and technologies that are often one-time costs. Innovation goes beyond something new and exciting and can often be a change to a current process or experience. These costs can turn into higher profits as they improve employee performance, align processes or add value to the customer experience. This can be a very persuasive tool when presenting the innovation to stakeholders or outside investors. While identification of the cost, benefits and return on investment of the innovation can be daunting, keep in mind that the more informed you are about the cost and benefits, the better equipped you are in presenting the innovation to the stakeholders.

Research foundations

Innovation has an impact on large, medium, small and entrepreneurial levels. There are many different ways to fund innovation depending on the business level, financial supporter or the innovation itself (Kasper, 2014). The internal policies and procedures of a business or corporation also have major impacts on the ability to fund an innovation (Spiceland, 2011). Factoring internal or external funding as well as the impact of the funding needed comes into consideration when approaching funding. However these can be broken down into four different basic levels:

- Internal funding – Small financial impact
- Internal funding – Medium financial impact
- Internal funding – Large financial impact
- External funding – Any amount

Innovations that have small financial impacts are more easily funded but can take just as much effort in achieving. Some businesses are able to absorb this type of expense in annual or quarterly budgets and without senior management approval. Not all innovations carry a financial impact that is outside of the normal functional duty of an area or individual and may not include the need for financing (Spiceland, 2011). In these instances, the need to obtain additional funds may not be necessary. However, if funding is required the same steps may be needed for obtaining the funds.

Innovations that have medium financial impact may require a higher level of approval based on the intricacies of the project. The more funding that is needed the more likelihood of additional approval. The funding may require investing activities and financing activities (Spiceland, 2011). Most corporations or businesses have approval limits for certain management staff. For example, a senior manager may have a signing limit of 100,000, while a vice president may have a signing limit of 1,000,000 and so on. Only the business itself can determine the level of financial impact and the funding that the innovation requires.

Innovations that have large financial impacts will require senior management approval or higher. Additionally, depending on the true financial impact may also require the business to add the capital expense to its regulatory reporting on a quarterly or annual basis (Atkins, 2007). A large financial impact has to be presented with a financial plan and a risk assessment. The impact of the risk is extremely important to whether or not the innovation can progress. This is why the CBA and the ROI become so important (Atkins, 2007).

External funding and entrepreneurial funding can be approached for different reasons. The business may not be large enough to fund the innovation without outside assistance or the business is a startup and seed money is needed (Goodman, 2016: 62). External funding may also require a business plan to prove the effectiveness of the current business and to present the potential for a startup. Having the ability to demonstrate that an innovation has a high potential to be a success allows for more opportunities of funding (Lewandowska, 2013).

There are many means of achieving external funding, for example loans, venture capital, equity funding, and even crowd funding (Galope, 2014). Loans come in many forms depending upon the size of the business and the stability of the business. These include loans such as new business, small business, personal or equity, to name a few (Gitman, 2012). Financial institutions require underwriting (the process to verify that the borrower meets requirements set by the financial institution), which may include examinations of the financial status of the business, past credit history, potential collateral and the potential value of the innovation (Stevens-Huffman, 2012). Requirements vary by financial institution and can take several weeks for approval while the validity of the loan is evaluated.

Venture capital is an investment where individuals or businesses buy an interest in an idea where the innovator has already had success but wants to expand that success (Lewandowska, 2013). The investor looks at the long-term growth potential of the innovation as part of the decision process. In some instances, a venture capital fund is managed by a venture capital firm and fund manager. A stakeholder (investor) utilizes the skill set of the fund manager to invest and determine the validity of a potential business opportunity (Draper, 2015). The firms can have investors from all over the world and foreign investment is a potential backer for innovation (Salkoff, 2015).

Equity funding is taking an interest in the business as an owner and can be more complex as it involves a percentage of the business the investor receives (Draper, 2015). The method potentially involves the selling of stocks to investors as a means of gaining interest of investors (Wonglimpiyarat, 2012). In equity funding the innovator needs to keep in mind that the investor is not only looking for a return on their investment, but also a solid hold on the financial future of the business overall. Keeping this in mind the inventor should carefully consider whether or not they are willing to give up a potential profit to an investor (Goodman, 2016).

Crowdfunding, while newer, is a means to an end by allowing multiple individuals to freely give funds to any given venture (Chan, 2017). It is a method to fund an innovation outside of traditional banking methods, rather utilizing public and personal connections instead (Ennsgraber, 2015). Crowdfunding itself involves a vast number of individual investors pooled from online internet users (Calvo, 2015). Hence it is commonly utilized on the entrepreneur level. A depth of research will be needed when utilizing crowdfunding to gain the most value from the funding method as there are many specialized crowdfunding sites that may be utilized.

Application and implementation strategies

With the clarification of what you've deemed necessary to finance the innovation you know need to understand your stakeholders. Who are the stakeholders? How does the innovation affect their bottom line? Since innovations can come from a multitude of different industries or prospects there are just as many stakeholders that can present. Additionally, the size of the innovation will also have an impact on the stakeholders. Most often if the innovation has a financial impact it will involve the Chief Financial Officer and in turn could involve the Chief Executive Officer. Other considerations need to be taken for the Chief Compliance Officer, Board of Directors and potentially stock holders. Each industry will drive who the stake holders will be.

Singh (2014) identified that stakeholders are just as important as the innovation itself as the influence of one stakeholder can move the interest of another. As well, if one stakeholder feels that the innovation is detrimental to their line of business this could cause dissention. This is why it is important to know your stakeholders and to identify them early on. There are different methods of identification as well as many sources that can provide you with guidance on who should be part of your presentation (Singh, 2014). Identification of the level of impact your innovation has is key. At what level of the organization does the idea impact, department, line of business, and business as a whole? Who are the key players in those areas? In some instances, you may have to present the idea to your direct management team prior to presenting it to senior management.

Some organizations are very large while others can consist of a small leadership teams. In the instance of small leadership teams the task can be less daunting but still requires understanding how each of the stakeholders is impacted by the innovation. On the other hand, larger groups of stakeholders may need to just understand the innovation and what the financial bottom line is. Either way, both must be treated with respect or a need to maintain a well-rounded understanding of the stakeholder is needed (Eskerod, 2016). Think about whom the innovation has an effect on, how do each of these individuals impact the success of the idea and who needs more information than others (Eskerod, 2016).

Keep in mind the project team is included in the list of stakeholders. While they may not be in the decision-making process of pursuing the innovation, they will in the end need to be on board to make the innovation a success. The project team is also responsible for keeping the project budget in line. Any issues with process or product can cause a financial impact. Having a solid plan that allows for potential issues such as these is prudent financially.

The stakeholders are a key part of getting the innovation funded. So how should you present your financial data to your stake holders? This can be achieved in many manners; however, your audience should be a key factor is how you present the data. Keep the financial data clear and unobscured. Make it easy to read or present and clear and concise. Present the data in manner that allows the stakeholder to see the overall picture with the ability to drive down to the level of detail that would provide a clear picture. These steps should help in presenting your data:

1   Financial Overview – Business Impact Statement – overall cost and overall benefit;
2   Breakdown – Cost (physical, technological, human and any other);
3   Breakdown – Benefits (policy, procedure, product, customer);
4   Return on Investment.

These should come after any information you are presenting on the innovation. Present the idea with positive impacts. Present the financial overview that gives a business impact statement. A business impact statement provides a strong foundation for presenting what the innovation can positively do for the business (Griffen, 2015). This is a perfect transition to the overall costs and then the overall benefits. By presenting the cost first you are able to counter potential disparity with the overall benefits. You may then go into breakdowns of the cost and benefits if needed. Finally, present the return on investment of what the innovation will bring to the stake holders. This leaves them with a positive view of what the innovation can do. In addition to presenting the above information remember who your audience is. For some the financial data is important, but it may not be as important as the effect the innovation has on a specific area. You may need to also discuss impacts to different areas or personnel. However, remember to present the data in a manner that is positive and reinforce them with the financial data.

Discussion

Financial data represents the core of the business, but the viewpoint of the business is its customers and values. Innovation leads to better customer experiences, cleaner processes and greater potential for gains. While a business is highly in tune with its clientele, it's the ability to service those clients with the most cost efficient means and services. Financial plans lead these changes and put constraints on what will or will not transpire in a process. Organizations and leaders often utilize formal processes for financing innovations. Innovation in today's business environment is not limited to one industry. In fact, many industries rely on innovations to maintain a competitive advantage. Specifically, financial gains made from innovations (Madsen, 2015). This is not different dependent upon the industry. The main focus for a business is the product and the bottom line.

However, there are some differences in approach based on technologies and on regulatory requirements, as well as where the company is based. Each industry is governed in some way by some sort of regulatory body. In this manner; there are differences in approaches to innovation related to a financial impact. Most of these are discussed based on the size of the business and the impact the business might have if it fails. One important thing to note is that not all innovation ideas come from inside the business itself. We can specifically look at the financial industry and the impact of innovation on banking. The banking industry looks toward innovation to drive its processes. On the other side, we can look at a mandated innovation from Europay, Mastercard and Visa (EMV) to maintain smart-chip based cards (Dahiya, 2014). The innovation was developed by the card industry and not by the banking industry yet it has a huge financial impact on the financial industry. Each financial institution that was impacted made the innovative change based on an outside impact. However, the point of the chip-based card was to deter fraud (Morrison, 2015). Thus, the cost benefit analysis would be driven by lower fraud rates (Dahiya, 2014).

With this example, you can see that innovations do not always come from inside a company. They can be mandated by industry leaders or government regulations. What doesn't change is the need to do the cost benefit analysis, the return on investment, the financial plan and the presentation to the leadership team. What might change is who on the business level champions the innovation. In this instance, it was left in the hands of product and compliance teams to achieve. Innovation can be inspired both inside and outside an individual business or industry. This means the financial impact can come from inside or outside the individual business or industry. Keeping the competitive advantage also means ensuring that trademarks, service marks and registrations have to be searched as do patents (Harding, 2016). This can require intervention from legal entities both inside and outside of the business. There are some industries that reluctantly make changes that are mandated. In other situations, delays occur due to the inability for an industry to quickly abide by a ruling or change required by someone outside the industry. Furthermore, there are times when changes are mandated and then revoked when it is realized that the industry can't make the change in the time frames promulgated. No matter what the industry, outside mandates will always transpire and therefore the means and knowledge to devise a financial plan is a necessity.

Summary

Innovations can present wonderful experiences for both the industry and the customer. In order to get the innovation realized there must be a foundation for funding. Taking the steps to identify the key costs associated with the innovation helps to substantiate the knowledge of the innovation leader in identification of expenses. The next step is to identify the benefits that the innovation will present. These are not only the innovation itself, but the positive impact on the business. One must not forget the return on the investment and its impact to the bottom line for the key stake holders. Understanding the steps a business must take to acquire funding is one step in development of the financial plan. Presenting a financial plan along with the innovation provides the stakeholders with a well-rounded picture of what the overall impact of the innovation is. It also provides the leadership team with the necessary information to make an informed decision on the risks that may be associated. As an innovation leader, being prepared with financial data and understanding who the stakeholders is a positive step to presenting the idea. Build upon what the idea is. Present a full picture of what will transpire and what the forward view will be. Focus on the benefits and use them to counter the costs. With a well laid financial forecast and identification of key points the financial plan can substantiate the validity of the innovation.

References

Arney, E, 2017, *Learning for Organizational Development*, Kogan Page, London, UK.
Atkins, A, Kaplan, R, Matsumura, E and Young, SM, 2007, *Management Accounting*, 5th edn, Prentice Hall, New Jersey, USA.

Bendle, N and Bagga, C, 2016, 'The metrics that marketers muddle', *MIT Sloan Management Review.*

Calvo, S, 2015, 'Funding characteristics of an established crowdfunding platform', *Michigan Journal of Business*, vol. 8, no. 1, pp. 11–46.

Chan, C and Parhankangas, A, 2017, 'Crowdfunding innovative ideas: How incremental and radical innovativeness influence funding outcomes', *Entrepreneurship: Theory & Practice*, vol. 41, no. 2, pp. 237–263.

Dahiya, R, 2014, 'Getting ready for EMV', *Independent Banker*, vol. 64, no. 6, pp. 68–70.

Draper, A, 2015, 'You're gonna need a bigger boat: Strategies for funding business innovation without biting off more than you can chew', *Governance Directions*, vol. 67, no. 5, pp. 278–281.

Ennsgraber, C, Grabmann, E and Lehner, O, 2015, 'Entrepreneurial implications of crowdfunding as alternative funding source for innovations', *Venture Capital*, vol. 17, no. 1–2, pp. 171–189.

Eskerod, P and Jepsen, A, 2016, *Project Stakeholder Management*, Routledge, London.

Galope, R, 2014, 'What types of start-ups receive funding from the Small Business Innovation Research (SBIR) Program?', *Journal Technology Management Innovation*, vol. 9, no. 2, pp. 17–28.

Gitman, LJ and Zutter, CJ, 2012, *Principles of Managerial Finance*, 13th edn, Prentice Hall, Boston.

Goodman, M, 2016, 'One bazillion potential shareholders', *Entrepreneur*, vol. 44, no. 7, pp. 58–63.

Griffen, M, 2015, *How to Write a Business Plan*, 5th edn, American Management Association.

Harding, S, 2016, 'Meet the patents: Fostering innovation and reducing costs by opening patent portfolios', *Journal of Business & Technology Law*, vol. 11, no. 2, pp. 199–217.

Hwang, K, 2015, 'Cost-benefit analysis: its usage and critiques', *Journal of Public Affairs*, vol. 16, no. 1, pp. 75–80.

Kasper, G and Marcoux, J, 2014, 'The re-emerging art of funding innovation', *Stanford Social Innovation Review*, vol. 12, no. 12, pp. 28–35.

Leong, K, Tan, W and Leong, E, 2014, *Venture Capital*, Marshall Cavendish International, Asia.

Lewandowska, L, 2013, 'Opportunities for funding innovation', *Comparative Economic Research*, vol. 16, no. 4, pp. 57–78.

Madsen, T and Leiblen, M, 2015, 'What factors affect the persistence of an innovation advantage?', *Journal of Management Studies*, vol. 52, no. 8, pp. 1097–1127.

Moffett, M, Stonehill, A and Eiteman, D, 2009, *Fundamentals of Multinational Finance*, 3rd edn, Pearson/Prentice Hall, Boston.

Morrison, D, 2015, 'Card fraud relief awaits EMV arrival', *Credit Union Times*, vol. 26, no. 10, pp. 1–17.

O'Brien, J, 2015, *Category Management in Purchasing*, 3rd edn, Kogan Page, London, UK.

Salkoff, B, 2015, 'Sparking new business: US innovation, with Chinese funding, Chinese', *China Business Review*, p. 1.

Singh, H, 2014, *Mastering Project Human Resource Management: Effectively Organize and Communicate with All Project Stakeholders*, Pearson Financial Times Press, London, UK.

Spiceland, JD, Sepe, JF and Nelson, MW, 2011, *Intermediate Accounting*, 6th edn, McGraw-Hill Irwin, New York, USA.

Stevens-Huffman, L, 2012, 'Growth opportunity', *Smart Business Los Angeles*, vol. 1, no. 10, pp. 24.

Weimer, DL and Vining, AR, 2011, *Policy Analysis: Concepts and Practice*, 5th edn, Longman Publishing Group, New York.

Wonglimpiyarat, J, 2012, 'Equity financing and capital market funding policies to support entrepreneurial development in Asia: Comparative cases of Thailand, Malaysia, Singapore, and Taiwan', *Journal of Private Equity*, vol. 15, no. 4, pp. 10–24.

Part II

Innovation leadership success stories

7 Today I fly!

The extraordinarily innovative Diavolo Dance Company

Jonathan Gangi

What makes art compelling? What makes art impactful and transformative? What gives arts products the power to provide audiences with memorable aesthetic experiences? The answer to this question for the dance company, Diavolo, originates in the creative process used to develop their distinctive style of dance works. This process is very innovative for a dance company and is the foundational core of all of Diavolo's organizational activity. From an inspirational idea to actualization, Diavolo's process is a wonderful example of how innovation leadership can work in any organization, and as such, is the primary concept of this chapter.

This story shows how an artist, Jacques Heim, led the formation of a dance company based on who he was, what he knew, and whom he knew (Sarasvathy, 2008), and demonstrates how an innovation leader can form a vision that resonates with partners who bring additional talent to the venture. These self-selecting partners play an invaluable role in co-creating successful products and an entire organization. Heim's passion for his work and his ability to empower others to help achieve and shape his vision illustrates how innovation leadership principles can profoundly impact an arts organization and the many people within its sphere of influence. The goal of this chapter is to serve as a valuable link between multiple disciplines by presenting artistic processes and approaches to innovation leadership, allowing those from other fields to glean insights that may otherwise be difficult to observe, absorb, and implement.

Description

The creative process of Diavolo demonstrates how the CREATE Model, the two types of innovation (exploratory and value-added innovation), and two fundamental leadership theories (path-goal theory and leader-member exchange theory) manifest in an arts organization. The unraveling of this process is informative and inspiring as these elements are interwoven, interdependent, and non-obvious. The formation of Diavolo's innovation leaders, the levels at which new ideas are generated, and the sources of innovation all spring from the core values of trust, teamwork, honesty, integrity, discipline, hard work, and overcoming fear.

The thesis of this chapter is that Diavolo's creative process and approach to leading innovation can be adopted and implemented by organizations in any industry. Key points can be applied within organizations in the following ways. As a founder and innovation leader, achieving organizational goals without compromising personal and organizational vision is possible through creative thinking. For example, Jacques initially spent a year researching dance companies in the USA to determine if others produced something that would compete with his desire to create a dance company and product that combined his love of architecture, movement, and dance in a unique, meaningful, and engaging way with the goal of providing audiences with memorable aesthetic experiences.

Seemingly immovable barriers should be examined from all angles before giving up and innovation leaders at all levels can benefit from this type of thinking. For example, a major perceptual barrier for many artists is the belief that taking action to make money with art means that they must compromise their artistic/aesthetic vision for their work and this is often viewed as an immovable barrier. It seems the choice is either fulfilling one's artistic vision through the art that is produced or creating something according to current trends and popular taste so that it will sell.

Organizations and innovation leaders of all kinds can learn from the improvisational, co-creative process and practice of creating artistic work. For example, organizations and innovation leaders can emulate the artistic process of throwing away preconceptions about new products and allowing creative ideas to emerge. This happens through creating a fluid environment characterized by flexible and adaptable thinking that is not fearful of extended periods of change and ambiguity. A discussion of innovation and creativity within arts organizations inherently involves grappling with the following questions. What does innovation mean in this context? What is most important during the product development phase? How is the risk and success of an innovative artistic product measured?

Johansson (2006) describes innovation as something new and valuable. Many artists and arts leaders would agree with this characterization, however, determining the value of something as subjective in nature as artistic work is challenging. Stoneman (2010) introduces the concept of *soft innovation*, which includes aesthetic, artistic, sensory, and intellectual products and services whose significance cannot and should not be judged according to functional, utilitarian uses. As an economist, he considers the financial impact of soft innovation to be a factor in determining if new products and services are significant or valuable. Not all artists and leaders of arts organizations would agree with this perspective as other types of impact create value and significance as well; for instance social/cultural, emotional, and artistic/aesthetic impact.

When creating new work, Hirschman (1983) points out that artists can orient their creativity towards a variety of audiences, such as the self, peers/industry professionals, and the public at large based upon a variety of objectives, such as self-expression, recognition/acclaim, and money. These choices for artists and leaders of arts organizations illustrate the many tensions within arts industries because creating for the self can produce high levels of intrinsic satisfaction for artists and presenting this work can significantly help to achieve an organization's artistic mission and vision. However, artistic work of this kind may not yield financial rewards and is more likely to have a smaller pecuniary impact. In this case, only two of the triple-bottom line goals for nonprofit arts organizations (economic necessity, artistic quality, and broad public access) would be achieved (Wyszomirski, 2013).

As a nonprofit art organization, the story of Diavolo involves all of these tensions. How is the artistic vision of Jacques realized during the creation of new dance works? Does he create for himself, his peers in the dance world, for the public at large, or simply to make large financial profits? How does Diavolo achieve its mission as nonprofit while at the same time sustaining a sufficient operating budget? How does innovation leadership happen in this context? The next section answers these questions by providing a backstage pass into the world of Diavolo.

The story

Diavolo Dance Company, founded in 1992 by Artistic Director Jacques Heim, has existed for twenty-five years. The name Diavolo, meaning "Today I Fly", is partially inspired by the Spanish word for "day" and the Latin word for "I fly." As a groundbreaking acrobatic dance company, the name is a lively description and summary of their unique performance style. During the company's first seven years of existence, Jacques focused on the formation of his artistic vision, ideas about the kind of work he wanted to create, and developing what would become his innovative approach to choreography as an architect of motion. Other than its European debut at the 1995 Edinburgh Fringe Festival, which began the formation of Diavolo's international reputation as a cutting-edge dance company, performances took place mostly in Los Angeles. In 1999, the company embarked upon its first major tour of North America, and since then, has been touring nationally and internationally for the past eighteen years.

Although Jacques is fascinated with movement, dance, architecture and structures, he is not a dancer himself and has no formal training in architecture. He spent time as a student at the California Institute of the Arts and has a background as a street performer. From the time of his undergraduate years at Cal Arts, Jacques knew he wanted to start a dance company that utilized structures. His artistic language of architecture and movement developed out of his love for props and large structures.

In 1992, Heim researched dance companies to determine if there were other companies in the USA using the language of architecture in motion. Knowing that American dance companies have a difficult time of drawing audiences, in comparison to other art forms, he wanted to be sure that he could offer audiences something different and unique. His research revealed that very few dance companies were using the language of architecture in motion. Some companies utilized props, but not the very particular language of architecture in motion. The research confirmed to Jacques that there was an opportunity in the USA for the type of dance company he wanted to launch, thus, he founded Diavolo.

During the early years of Diavolo, Jacques was invited to work with the University of California-Los Angeles dance program. In this role, he taught dancers how to physically interact with structures and moving objects. Diavolo's core values of trust, teamwork, honesty, integrity, discipline, hard work, and overcoming fear, started very early on in the life of Diavolo, prior to Jacques teaching at UCLA. However, working with UCLA's dance program helped to test and refine the foundational philosophy, mission, and technique of Diavolo. A primary core value involves the dancers, as teammates, trusting each other. As a dancer working for an acrobatic dance company that performs on moving structures, trust is incredibly important. If the dancers do not trust each other when physically interacting with other moving dancers and sets, structures, and props, the artistic vision for the dance piece will both literally and figuratively fall flat, and fail.

Honesty and integrity are also crucial. If a dancer claims to be strong enough to execute a dangerous jump or catch another dancer falling from a moving wall, then another team member's physical safety could be at risk if they are not telling the truth. Clearly, teamwork, discipline, hard work, and overcoming fear are also very important values for all dancers to commit to and live out. Those who are not true to themselves and true to the company, who do not believe in Diavolo's core values, are asked to leave the organization.

Jacques navigates the tensions between creating artistic work according to his vision, satisfying public taste, and the need to make money in an exemplary manner. During Diavolo's first national tour in 1999, Jacques would sit in the audience during performances to monitor audience reactions. During these observations, Jacques realized the audience was quite surprised that Diavolo's offerings were categorized as dance. He noticed that they were attracting an audience that typically could not relate to dance but were fascinated with the very visual and visceral nature of his work. This confirmed that his artistic intuition resonates very strongly with at least certain segments of dance audiences, and those who normally would not attend dance performances.

Heim is very aware that international presenters will not pay large sums of money to hire his company to perform if he creates work that is simply nice and regular. They could hire a local company to perform predictable work for a lower cost. Thus, he creates new work that will be of interest to presenting organizations around the globe. By knowing his competition, Jacques creates new work that is innovative and unique in the dance world. This increases the likelihood that presenting organizations will pay to bring Diavolo performances to international venues.

Jacques deals with the riskiness of new artistic work by following his artistic instincts and surrounding himself with a great creative team. He also remains humble and approaches every new piece as if it were the first time creating and directing a piece, as if he knows nothing. Additionally, he conducts private showings of the new work at various stages of development with the goal of receiving feedback from a representative sample of potential audiences.

He creates based on his intuition when developing the theme of a new piece, but also keeps in mind that he is creating for an international audience. For Jacques, knowing that the work is going to be international causes him to create differently and to consider the bigger picture. This approach shifts his focus from creating only for local audiences to creating new dance pieces that appeal to national and international audiences including audiences that know nothing about dance. Yet, he creates something that is still very meaningful, visual, visceral, and remains true to the philosophy and language of architecture in motion.

Thus, the result is a creative approach that balances the tensions of creating high quality artistic work, fulfilling the aesthetic vision of the creative artist, creating with a particular audience in mind, and the goal of making money. Jacques' approach is successful, as evidenced by Diavolo's international touring schedule and audience feedback. Attendees comprising the dance enthusiast segment, although they have never seen anything like Diavolo, say the combination of elements is fascinating and feels different. Other audiences, especially those who normally do not attend dance performances, love Diavolo's refreshing fusion of architecture, movement, and dancers. Innovation in the creative industries generates increased demand from consumers who are not typically drawn to a certain product (Caves, 2000). In fact, many audience members prefer Diavolo because it is not like typical dance companies.

The people who comprise Diavolo's dance team bring a variety of abilities, experience, and training to the company. For example, some are trained ballet dancers, some are gymnasts, and still others are actors, rock climbers, and even stunt doubles for movie studios. Diavolo's creative process is atypical for a dance company and very innovative. Many dance companies treat dancers as performers only, not collaborators in the creative process, and would never ask for their opinion about the choreography or other elements of a new piece. This richness and variety of background training and experience provides a broad scope of ideas and inputs as the dancers, together with Jacques, co-create the story and choreography of a new work.

For Heim, collaboration, interconnectivity, and relationships are vital to his work and process. He highly values and utilizes a creative team, comprised of a sculptor/architect, set designers, engineers, a musical composer, a spoken word artist, a lead choreographer, and dramaturge. When working with the team, Jacques is able to communicate his vision for a new dance work and inspire others to help create the new product by bringing their unique skills, knowledge, and talents to the improvisational process.

Heim's creative process for new dance pieces begins with a passionate idea. This idea could come from a moving experience with artwork of some kind or from observing people interacting on the street. He is fascinated by human reactions to physical objects and the impact and influence of structures upon human behavior. Jacques stores his ideas and inspirations in a dream book; a type of journal in which he draws initial sketches for structures or sets that the dancers perform on that relate to an inspirational passionate idea.

In general, Jacques is able to fulfill his artistic vision despite financial constraints. However, the cost of materials used to create the physical structures does impact his vision in terms of size and scope. He cannot always create the structures he envisions due to size constraints of most venues' stages and the cost of creating such large-scale structures causing Diavolo's performance fee to become too expensive for many presenting organizations. Thus, in some instances, financial and practical considerations do present challenges to Jacques' artistic vision.

A new piece requires Jacques to research many different architects and types of architecture as the basis of his inspiration. He creates drawings and then works with his sculptor/architect over a period of months to make a small model of the set structures based upon his initial drawings of the concept. By the first day of rehearsal, Jacques knows exactly how the piece starts and ends and has a book with all of the scenes. Prior to the first rehearsal, he will meet with the dancers and give them homework to do their own research on movement. This results in better quality collaborations during studio rehearsals in terms of the meaning, movement, and substance of the new work.

Using a structured improvisational process, Jacques has the dancers play with the set, structure, and props for at least a six-week period. This allows for testing and experimentation in terms of what the structure can do and what it needs to do, while at the same time, developing narrative for the new work. This process can take more than six weeks and, in some instances, the story and the structure changes dramatically from his initial ideas. Jacques greatly values the varied time frames and new directions as it helps him to let go of any preconceptions that he may have brought into the process and allows innovations to take shape.

This structured improvisational process highlights Jacques's approach to leading innovation. Simply by being members of the company, the dancers know that the language of Diavolo is very collaborative. As self-selecting partners, they understand that they are expected and encouraged to provide creative input. Thus, throughout the entire rehearsal process, the dancers provide input pertaining to the choreography and collaboratively create the movements with a lead choreographer. For example, when they start rehearsing a scene, Jacques asks his creative team to consider each moment of the piece by saying, "What is that moment?" Then they talk about it. Someone will say, "Ok, if that is what this moment is supposed to be, how do we make that moment? What is the theme of that moment?" Another will say, "How do we feel about it? How do we want to make the audience feel?" After these questions are discussed, one person suggests they start moving in a certain manner very slowly. Then, they say, "Ok, how slowly, backwards, forwards? Ok, let's try it and see how it goes. Start doing it. Ok, play a little bit with that."

Jacques wants, needs, and encourages creative input regarding the intent and content of every moment and every scene. Together, the team envisions and evaluates and during every step of the process considers how each moment emotionally impacts the artists and the audience. They are very concerned that they put themselves in the position of an audience member so as not to lose them. The goal is to create from the point of view of the person who is watching for the first time. Through this structured process of improvisation, Diavolo is able to consider the audience during the creative process while producing innovative artistic work that is true to Jacque's artistic vision and the organization's mission.

The dancers of Diavolo are required to have nerves of steel because they manipulate the structure while rehearsing, starting scenes from the beginning over and over again. At times, the structure can be heavy, cumbersome, difficult, and dangerous. In some instances, the structure breaks down and must be repaired, requiring the dancers wait long periods of time before moving again. They, at times, get hurt by the structure and then receive medical attention to patch and stitch the wounds and, once completed, return to rehearsal. The men and women of Diavolo are required to have incredible levels of patience and to be like gladiators, as they are dancers, collaborators, and creators while at the same time they must function in part like construction workers, scientists, mathematicians, and logicians.

Discussion

The argument of this chapter is that Jacques Heim's creative process and approach to leading innovation can be adopted and implemented by organizations in any industry. Diavolo's story enacts the principles of two fundamental leadership theories: path-goal theory and leader-member exchange theory. Path-goal theory of leadership is concerned with how leaders influence the way subordinates view their work goals, personal goals, and the path to attain these goals (House, 1975). Jacques' passion for his dance company is compelling and infectious. His creative team is motivated by his incredible artistic vision and aesthetic taste, and the way that he empowers them to contribute to the process. The dancers are self-selecting members of the team and are committed to the core values of the company. As such, their goals are inherently similar to Jacques' and they work towards creating compelling dance works. The dancers have the goal of becoming and remaining professional dancers and Jacques clarifies their path to that goal by articulating clear core values for the company. As the innovation leader, Heim provides motivating and satisfying work environments for his dancers by encouraging their creative input when developing new pieces, as well as providing an opportunity for them to perform.

Leader-member exchange theory deals with the developmental relationship between leaders and followers (Lunenburg, 2010). The members of Heim's creative team work with him on an individual basis. Due to Jacques' preference to work collaboratively with people who provide the skills that he lacks, followers naturally take on greater levels of responsibility, receive significant amounts of personal attention, and must be able to function with greater amounts of autonomy and freedom in their roles. This type of culture yields intrinsic rewards, because individuals are valued for their creativity and expertise, and extrinsic rewards such as public recognition, acclaim, and financial compensation. For the dancers specifically, it is incredible to participate creatively in the development of new dance works rather than simply executing movements as directed.

Diavolo's creative process includes the steps in the CREATE Model. For example, Jacques introduces an initial inspirational idea to the creative team and they add to this through the structured improvisational process. When Heim leads by considering each moment and scene in terms of how both the dancers and the audience will respond, he is supporting idea generation by encouraging input from everyone. Jacques and his team identify, evaluate, and implement innovative ideas as they improvise, while remaining open to making any necessary changes.

When creating new dance works using structured improvisation, Diavolo is using exploratory innovation, which involves generating brand new ideas. There are times, however, when Jacques and his creative team will rework older pieces. In this case, Diavolo is using value-added innovation, which involves modifying and improving existing ideas. Regardless of the type of innovation used, there are risks involved when developing new products. In the performing arts, risk involves both artistic and financial considerations (Colbert, 2012). A consumer's perception of risk is heightened by the fear that they may not enjoy or understand the new performing arts product (Crealey, 2003).

Jacques' approach to innovation leadership helps Diavolo to limit these risks. For example, they are able to keep their audience in mind during the creation of new work. This reduces the risk of products that do not resonate with an audience. However, the artistic vision and creative spark in the work is not diminished by this approach. Heim has learned to trust his creative intuition and creates in a way that balances achieving artistic goals and connecting with audiences to reduce financial risks.

Another tactic Jacques uses to reduce risk, as mentioned previously, is to offer private showings of new work at various stages of development in order to receive feedback from potential audience members. This feedback is another way to evaluate innovative ideas and products and lead innovation, and is similar to the build-measure-learn feedback loop described in the Lean Startup method (Ries, 2011). Diavolo's creative team brings a depth and breadth of knowledge, skill, and perspective to the new product development method that can process and interpret the feedback in a way that achieves resonance with audiences in an authentic way. Thus, the way Jacques leads innovation by empowering his creative team is not only brilliant, but can be copied by innovation leaders in any organization and industry (House, 1975; Lunenburg, 2010).

Heim, as an individual is certainly an innovation leader. However, his creative team, can also be described as a group within an organization that leads innovation. As such, the levels at which new ideas are generated and the sources of innovation within Diavolo include the individual level and group level. Leader-member exchange theory suggests that leaders form high-quality, trust, and respect-based relationships with followers (Bauer, 2016). Jacques achieves this by articulating a clear set of core values asking creative team members to commit to the core values and then gives them the space to contribute creatively. These are core principles that leaders in any industry could adopt and apply as they lead innovation within their organizations.

Summary

The key points from this innovation leadership success story can be applied within organizations in the following ways. As a founder and innovation leader, achieving organizational goals without compromising personal and corporate vision is possible through creative thinking. For those working in arts organizations, the story of Diavolo demonstrates that it is possible to fulfill organizational goals without compromising artistic vision. For artists, Jacques' approach shows that considering the market and competitors prior to creating aesthetic products can be a successful strategy.

Organizations and innovation leaders can learn from the improvisational, co-creative process, and practices of Diavolo. This process engages the founder/innovation leader and team members in a journey of testing and co-creation, exploring possibilities, and cultivating the product together. This creative process involves flexibility in terms of time, as the product may morph in entirely new directions. Preconceptions must be thrown away to allow innovations to emerge because product development is never static and products will change, sometimes even radically, over time.

Jacques is considered an effective director and leader because he asks his team to share and to trust (Goleman, 2002). His ability to collaborate with his creative team is the reason for Diavolo's success. His inspiration, artistic vision, and approach to innovation leadership has enabled him to launch and sustain a successful dance company. People are drawn to Diavolo because Jacques' artistic work is incredibly beautiful, emotionally moving, and exudes a transformative energy and experience.

References

Bauer, TN and Erdogan, B, 2016, 'Leader-Member Exchange (LMX) Theory: An Introduction and Overview', in TN Bauer and B Erdogan (eds), *The Oxford Handbook of Leader-Member Exchange*, pp. 3–8. Oxford University Press, Oxford.
Caves, RE, 2000, *Creative Industries: Contracts between Art and Commerce*, Harvard University Press, Boston, MA.
Colbert, F, 2012, *Marketing Culture and the Arts*, 4th edn. HEC, Montreal.

Crealey, M, 2003, 'Applying New Product Development Models to the Performing Arts: Strategies for Managing Risk', *International Journal of Arts Management*, vol. 5, no. 3, pp. 24–33.

Goleman, D, Boyatzis, RE and Mckee, A, 2002, *Primal Leadership: Realizing the Power of Emotional Intelligence*, Harvard Business School Press, Boston, MA.

Hirschman, EC 1983, 'Aesthetics, Ideologies and the Limits of the Marketing Concept', *Journal of Marketing*, vol. 47, no. 3, pp. 45–55.

House, RJ, and Mitchell, TR, 1975, *Path-goal Theory of Leadership*, Washington University Department of Psychology, Seattle.

Johansson, F, 2006, *The Medici Effect: What Elephants and Epidemics Can Teach Us About Innovation*, Harvard Business School Press, Boston, MA.

Lunenburg, FC, 2010, 'Leader-Member Exchange Theory: Another Perspective on the Leadership Process', *International Journal of Management, Business, and Administration*, vol. 13, no. 1, pp. 1–5.

Ries, E, 2011, *The Lean Startup: How Today's Entrepreneurs Use Continuous Innovation to Create Radically Successful Businesses*, Crown Business, New York.

Sarasvathy, SD, 2008, *Effectuation: Elements of Entrepreneurial Expertise*, Edward Elgar, Northhampton, MA.

Stoneman, P, 2010, *Soft Innovation: Economics, Product Aesthetics, and the Creative Industries*, Oxford University Press, Oxford.

Wyszomirski, MJ, 2013, 'Shaping a Triple-bottom Line for Nonprofit Arts Organizations: Micro-, Macro-, and Meta-policy Influences', *Cultural Trends*, vol. 22, nos. 3–4, pp. 156–166.

8   An innovation success in the private sector

Walter Robb and Mike Erdman

This chapter presents both large and small innovation successes in the private sector. The most significant innovation is associated with the development of a highly advanced CAT (Computerized Axial Tomography) scanner that shook the marketplace and established General Electric (GE) as the standard in the industry. This chapter will explore several other shorter stories of innovation success. Each of these stories highlights an innovation success that is based on the key elements of a successful innovation leader, which include the ability to recognize opportunities, having the courage to define a challenging and engaging future state that others will buy into, gathering and motivating the needed team of supporters, and demonstrating determination to achieve the lofty goals. We are confident that you will find examples of how some of the innovation leadership principles that are described in the earlier chapters of this book have been put to use to improve both company performance and that of individuals.

Description

Dr. Walter Robb, an up-and-coming manager at GE, was assigned to head up Medical System Division, a portion of the company that was not making a profit and was being considered for divestiture. Shortly after arriving, he learned that the business was being threatened by a new imaging technology, a CAT scanner. A competing company, EMI, was grabbing the market with its four-minute scanner and more than a dozen competitors announced that they were developing a two-minute scanner. Dr. Robb did not want to be a late to market manufacturer of a two-minute scanner, which was potentially a path to low market share. He pondered what would distinguish his struggling Medical Systems Division in this growing market-place.

Working with the GE Research & Development Center, he decided to challenge the GE team to develop a revolutionary scanner; one that would not require the patient to literally hold their breath for two minutes while the scan is performed. In fact, he tasked them with developing a five-second scanner; a technology that would require new mathematical models and detectors that were a fraction of the size of the then-current models. They delivered the prototype unit in 18 months to stay ahead of any developments by competitors. The market was ecstatic for the innovation. In three years, it went from an idea to orders in excess of $65,000,000. GE gained a leadership position with 50% of the CAT scanner market.

This is the story of this amazing turnaround; a turnaround that was founded in an audacious challenge, innovation leadership, and commitment promulgated throughout the organization and its suppliers. This story will provide a fascinating case study on innovation leadership. Likewise, it will provide some life-lessons that can help individuals identify and realize their potential. Dr. Robb led the GE Medical Systems Division to new heights throughout his career. In positions ranging from a Research Scientist to the Senior Vice President of Corporate Research and Development, he grew a number of innovations from obscurity to $2 billion in sales. And, he did this while still providing time to enjoy his growing family.

The story

The secret that made Dr. Robb so successful is not found in many modern business books. From the very beginning of his career as a Research Scientist, he did more than required to succeed on his projects. He was not reluctant to ask for the next position or what he could do to improve his chances for promotion. On many of his projects, there were times when taking a risk was an option. He usually took that risk. He did not always succeed, but when he did, the rewards for his organization and for him personally were worth the risk. The innovations that Dr. Robb led were not just in technical disciplines, but also in business management, marketing, and manufacturing. In industry, there are opportunities for bright, aggressive, and articulate individuals and the successful innovation leader has the courage and self-confidence to pursue these opportunities.

Dr. Robb's first general management position was to lead a start-up operation that grew to $7 million in sales. It prepared him to take on the role of General Manager of the GE Silicone Products division. As Dr. Robb turned his attention to his sales force, it became apparent that their 50-person sales staff could not compete with Dow Corning, who had 50 distributors helping their sales force sell equivalent products. Dr. Robb's sales managers had succeeded in finding another 50 distributors in the country that were prepared to challenge Dow Corning.

Likewise, Dr. Robb supported the development of an incentive program that included a kick-off meeting for the Presidents of the 50 distributors estimated to cost GE $50,000. Dr. Robb told the Sales Manager to proceed with the two-day meeting at a conference center in the Midwest and it was a huge success and sales increased. All 50 distributors were successful with the incentive program and sales jumped by more than 40% to $67 million. The increased sales generated a very significant profit and, as the newest GM in a corporation of 50 General Managers, Dr. Robb was recognized at the GE management meeting as someone who was willing to take a risk.

A year later Dr. Robb was asked to take over a larger division called GE Medical Systems. It specialized in making x-ray equipment for hospitals and clinics. It was about equal in sales to Picker, but both US companies were being challenged by Siemens, Philips and Toshiba. All of the competitors were more or less selling the same product. Unfortunately, GE's business had become unprofitable and, when Jack Welsh gave Dr. Robb the assignment, his last directive was to advise him, within a year, why GE should not sell the business. Taking this assignment was a risk, but Jack assured Dr. Robb that if the business was sold, there were other GM positions available for him.

A new company, EMI, was entering the medical imaging business with a form of x-ray equipment never seen before. It was called Computerized Axial Tomography (CAT) and the goal was to better differentiate various tumor entities in the human body. Initially it was limited to tumors in the brain. In their first year, EMI produced 12 units that they sold at a fraction of their production cost to the top 12 medical schools in the world. These systems required clamping the head of the patient during the 4½ minutes required to image one scan of the brain. A typical procedure would usually consist of imaging 4–6 scans, which meant that the patient's head was held in place for more than half an hour. It was worth that time, effort and expense to find a brain tumor, but it was incredibly uncomfortable and difficult to maintain positioning for an accurate image.

The response of the radiology community exceeded expectations and by early the next year, EMI had over 100 orders at $375,000 each. This success got the attention of existing x-ray companies and entrepreneurial scientists who saw the need for computer processing as equally important as the generation of an x-ray beam. Thirteen companies announced they would have systems that would reduce the scan time per scan to two minutes. The engineering team at GE Medical Systems also concluded that, to remain competitive, it was time to develop a two-minute-per-scan CAT as quickly as possible and with estimated completion in 18 months. While the total scan time was reduced using the new two-minute system, the patient's head still had to be held immobile for multiple scans.

Looking to capitalize on the strength of GE's Research and Development division, the Medical Systems division in Milwaukee asked GE research scientists in Schenectady if they had any suggestions for this project. Much to the surprise of the Milwaukee engineers and management, a research scientist described an entirely different design involving a fan-beam of x-ray detectors containing hundreds of x-ray detectors in a frame that would rotate around the patient's head and not back and forth as was the case with the current technologies. This device was far too complicated for the system which EMI had conceived in the 1960s. But, it had the advantage of permitting an image to be created in five seconds. The potential was huge, since with a short scan time, a patient would not be required to hold their breath while scanning the abdomen. In addition, the resolution was expected to be significantly improved. The Milwaukee team was excited with the idea. However, it was still an early research concept with the prototype not anticipated for five years. GE could not wait that long to get the product to market and pressure mounted to start on the much simpler two-minute prototype.

As the General Manager of GE Medical Systems, Dr. Robb was determined not to be the just another company making a two-minute scanner. He contacted the VP and Director of the GE R&D Center, regarding the dilemma. Would it be conceivable to build a fan-beam scanner in 18 months? After due consideration, the team in Schenectady not only said yes, but set project updates at six-month intervals to ensure the team was on track. Without hesitation, Dr. Robb took a huge risk and terminated all work on the two-minute scanner and cast the success of GE's CAT scan business on the Research Center's five second concept.

After meeting the first six-month objective of having a new x-ray detector invented that would make the fan-beam of over 300 detectors possible, GE's Milwaukee team got a boost in confidence that it might actually achieve its goal. In another six months, when the small five-inch diameter prototype was actually working, the enthusiasm regarding this being a huge breakthrough in imaging began to build. In an unprecedented move for GE, the Milwaukee team sent engineering and manufacturing personnel to Schenectady to begin designing a production scanner. They assumed the whole-body scanner would work. With six months still to go, the Milwaukee team started investing in a plant to produce the five-second scanner.

The goal for the first body image was set at 18 months from the start of development. The team achieved the goal, the prototype worked, and champagne was poured. Without question, this 18-month accomplishment is acknowledged as the fastest development of a breakthrough product that GE had ever seen. Two months later, Dr. Robb's team announced this achievement and invited 100 radiologists to see the scanner working in the GE R&D Center laboratory. Within months, half of these radiologists gave GE orders with a down payment of $100,000 on the half million-dollar system.

In the spring, a dinner was held near the R&D Center and 82 laboratory employees were recognized as having been key to the success of this project. The team had a timetable that few outside of the team had believed could be accomplished. In Milwaukee, another record was set; GE had a production CT scanner completed and working five months after the research prototype had been completed. The initial laboratory prototype was actually shipped to the Radiology Department at the University of California in San Francisco Hospital. While it did not perform perfectly and GE had the scare of having it possibly returned, these issues got resolved with the efforts of the Milwaukee and Schenectady labs. Thirteen scanners were sold the first year, 35 the next year, and well over 100 the year after. By then, GE had over 50% of the US scanner market even though several imaging companies had, by then, announced that their own fan-beam scanners were being produced.

With this success in America, GE Medical formed a joint venture in Japan and established marketing activities in the rest of the world. Within six years of the initial prototype, GE was getting over 50% of global CAT orders and other imaging companies were licensing the patents that GE possessed on the CT fan-beam, five-second scanner. The decision to terminate the development of a two-minute scanner and take a risk on the research lab developing a five-second scanner, was without question, the biggest risk Dr. Robb ever took. The hundreds of people who worked with Dr. Robb on that project remember the preceding four years being the happiest work experiences they have had. Employees worked far more hours than normally required. But, they could see that they were on track to have a huge breakthrough in medical imaging. A team spirit developed that helped accelerate progress at a rate much higher than would normally have occurred with a more modest goal. Team spirit not only saved the business, Dr. Robb and the team made GE Medical Systems the global leader in CAT technology, while introducing life-saving medical imaging technology never before available.

Forty years after the introduction of this scanner, it still represents the gold standard in CAT imaging. Gradual improvements have reduced the scan time to a fraction of a second and improved resolution by a factor of ten. The success of the GE CAT endeavor gave the Milwaukee team the confidence to count on another breakthrough from the Schenectady team when magnetic resonance imaging (MRI) was invented by two State University of New York (SUNY) professors. Once again using innovation leadership, the GE R&D Center produced the gold standard in MRI technology.

Discussion

The story above represents just one occasion where Dr. Robb took risks that paid off, both for his company as well as for him individually. Envisioning and taking audacious risks, demonstrating commitment, achieving organizational alignment, and team commitment were his keys to success in an industrial setting. Some other examples come to mind. During college, young Walt had occasions to help a professor and, in several cases, it had big payoffs.

In his junior year at Penn State, the Department Head of Chemical Engineering informed the class that they were responsible for planning and executing the chemical engineering demonstration for an annual engineering open house. He asked for two volunteers to be co-chairs of the committee. A good friend and Walt both raised their hands. It turned out that the friend had discovered a new girlfriend and was hopelessly distracted, so Walt had the burden of putting together the teams that were required. When it came time for Walt to apply to graduate school, the Department Head was his best reference. He even called the Chemical Engineering Department head at the University of Illinois and Walt ended up receiving a scholarship. In graduate school, Walt's adviser asked if anyone would volunteer to perform the complex calculations that would be required to support a new theory which he had created regarding dense gases around the critical point. Again, Walt offered to help, and for weeks worked on the calculations that resulted in two papers in *Physics Review*. The advisor very considerately named Walt as a co-author, and in addition, recommended him for one of the very few research fellowships available from companies. They were as beneficial as the teaching fellowships, but did not require grading papers, typical of a teaching assistant. For the two years that Walt worked on his Ph.D. thesis, he was able to concentrate full time on research. The key to success here was Walt's willingness to volunteer for additional, high visibility assignments.

There was another occasion when one of Dr. Robb's bosses asked him to stop by. His request was whether Dr. Robb was willing to take a three-month assignment with the GE Nuclear Division on a special study to be held in California. GE's leadership wanted to have one representative from the GE Research Lab on the team. Dr. Robb was probably not the first scientist whom he asked and the timing was not ideal. Dr. Robb and his wife were having their second child two weeks before the study was scheduled to begin. He really wanted to say yes, but knew he could not leave his wife back in Schenectady. He asked if the company would pay for his family's flights to and from California, as soon as they were comfortable traveling. The Nuclear Division agreed. The Robbs had a wonderful time in California, probably costing the company less travel money than it would have been charged if he had gone out alone with occasional trips back to Schenectady. Not too long after that, Dr. Robb's boss was given a promotion in the Chemical Division, and Dr. Robb was appointed as his successor. Taking the California assignment may have been critical to his getting the promotion. Helping your boss with a problem is almost always worthwhile, and taking special assignments often leads to new challenges and opportunities. Again, the key attributes of a successful innovation leader came into play in each of these examples. Seize opportunities, set engaging visions, and be tenacious in your work ethic.

Summary

While much of life follows a normal plan with small, well thought-out steps, sometimes you come to a crossroads or you are given an opportunity to do something extra and an important decision is required. Risks should not be taken without a thorough analysis and one should not expect a direct reward or *quid pro quo* for doing more. But, if some of these opportunities do not happen by themselves, do not wait for an opportunity to be presented to you. The following are some keys to being an innovation leader in business and industry. Volunteering for extra responsibilities, particularly those with high visibility/high payoff. Often these are high risk assignments where you often find opportunities for innovation. Recognize the triggers for innovation such as market drivers and opportunities to lead the organization in a new direction. Often you need to look where others have not gone. Establish a vision with a stretch, a new paradigm, or an audacious goal. Many people resist change, but the bold will join in your venture. Sell your vision and goal up, down, and across the organization. Differentiate between the now and the future state, identify the costs and benefits, and make the financial case for the investment. Have the personal courage to take calculated risks. Garner resources, both from within and outside of the organization to benefit from other perspectives. Pull together a diverse team of believers. Execute with passion and determination. If you really want to maximize your opportunities in life, expect that it will require doing a little more than what others think is necessary, and, on occasion, making a decision that may have some risk. Most significant gains do not get accomplished with a gradual approach, grab with gusto. And, best of all, it makes life rewarding and a lot more fun.

References

Robb, WL, 2014, *Taking risks: Getting ahead in business and life*, Meadow Brook Farm Publishing, Waukesha, WA.

9   Who's leading and who's learning?

R. Lee Viar IV

Several years ago, I had a student in my class who left an indelible impression on me. I was teaching a higher education, leadership, and policy course in a community college leadership doctoral program and a silver-haired gentleman walked into the classroom in a rather non-assuming manner. During the first two weeks of the course, he was extremely quiet, but very attentive. I started to initiate conversations with him during breaks and found him to be a fascinating person. I quickly realized that I was calling on him in the class more than he probably would have preferred.

I found that I was viewing the classroom differently than I had previously and started to lead all my classes in a different way due to his personal philosophy. Keep in mind, I am not a new professor. I have nearly two decades of experience in higher education, so this was very much a personal revolution. Because of this experience, I adopted a new leadership philosophy. I began viewing situations and issues through multiple lenses. I attempted to make the most complicated situation or scenario as basic as possible for those working with me. I viewed stress as being both productive and counter-productive and I remembered the importance of the audience. Let the learning begin for the professor.

Description

Leading from behind is not leading. It is merely following under the guise of leading. In higher education, why is there often an institutionalized focus on leading with outdated and archaic theories instead of leading innovation? The concept of learning should not be solely directed towards the students in the classroom. The ability to be open to innovation requires many in higher education to admit that they may not possess all of the answers and that students, both traditional and non-traditional, may possess valuable new ideas and creative concepts. Thus, for innovation in higher education to occur, a modicum of humility needs to be present. Can this truly take place in higher education? The answer is yes, but with a caveat; fear and egoism can cause an innovation to crumble in a blink of the eye. Many experts feel they have a significant mastery of their area of study. However, one obstacle to learning and developing innovations in a creative atmosphere may be the very individual leading the classroom, the professor. Fear can act as a deterrent to developing a culture of continuous innovation in a classroom. Fear, in academic environments, can be debilitating. History is full of people who have recognized the importance of stepping away from their own preconceived notions and embracing the perspectives of others. This change, as well as the development of an innovation, can happen in many different places: the battlefield, the board room, and even in my own classroom.

This chapter is a reflection and analysis of my own personal venture into this previously uncharted territory. I was confident of my own knowledge and skill set. I was trained and educated in such a manner that I was confident in my capability to reach my students, in my own way, of course. Yet, it took one senior learner in my evening class to educate me and provide me with the courage to be innovative in my teaching style as well as my approach to many aspects of my life. Was this an easy transformational experience? Absolutely not, because I was the professor and I had all the answers. This way of thinking was my first mistake and I needed renewal. Developing innovations in my thought process as an educator was truly transformational. I sincerely believe this experience will continue to enable me to grow as an educator and a person as well. No longer am I staying in my own swim lane. I am curious to see what is outside and how it can be applied to my classroom and students.

I often work with non-traditional students and this demographic is not always as interested in theory and concepts as it is in how the theories and concepts are applied practically in the workplace. Because of this, I stress an innovative mentality in my classroom. From day one, I state that we are going to learn this material together. Considering the audience that I am addressing, I ask my students to be willing to listen to what I am telling them based on my education and experiences, even though it may be contrary to what they have done in their personal and/or professional lives for years. How can I create a successful learning environment for my non-traditional students if I am not willing to admit that I also have something that I can learn from them? It is my goal and aspiration that, in this chapter, you will be able to connect the concept innovation leadership to your own experiences based on the stories of my previous students, subject matter experts in academia, business professionals, military leaders, and my own story.

The story

Higher education is a well-respected profession. History has shown that the better educated a society is, the more that it will prosper and thrive. The accomplishments of well-educated men and women are evident in every field of study. Yet, often, their vision of new or unique ideas is extremely myopic (Brookfield, 1995). My journey along the academic path took many twists and turns over the years, but I persevered despite a host of challenges. My self-perception was that I could work with and appreciate my students' lived experiences. Being an adult learner myself, I wanted a voice in my education and I wanted to offer the same to my students. I thought I was doing exactly that until, one evening, I realized that I had morphed into what I had been striving not to be. I had failed to fully embrace an academic strategy that Joshua Chamberlain created over a hundred years ago. Chamberlain felt pride in his innovative teaching methods in rhetoric and had developed entirely new ways of instruction which were very valuable to his students. He enjoyed it, counting none of it as drudgery, as his students responded and attended voluntary classes he organized. But, he met no encouragement from his superiors, only coldness and insistence that he continue some old methods of teaching (Trulock, 1992). However, these obstacles did not deter Chamberlain from blazing his own path by developing innovative strategies of reaching the students.

Being a novice historian, I have read dozens of books on the Civil War and World War II and I attempted to emulate many of the qualities of those that I had read about. For example, I greatly admire Admiral Chester Nimitz and how he dealt with the challenges of the mantle of command, training, and leading his men. However, it is not well-known that he served briefly as a professor. As a professor in California, Nimitz took a paternal and individual interest in each of his students. A few of the faculty were, at first, a little resentful of Nimitz. They earned their doctorates and, through the years of teaching and publishing, had made the slow climb from instructor to assistant professor to associate professor and had grown gray aspiring toward the rank of full professor. He could never understand why a master teacher should not be judged on the basis of his teaching skills and he never quite accepted the argument that the mastery of research, writing, and publishing solely provided a necessary background for teaching (Potter, 1976). I now believe that truly great leaders are not overly concerned with accolades. Instead, they focus on results accomplished by leading innovation and not being afraid of being different.

After talking on breaks in the hallway with my senior learner, his story inspired me to not be afraid of change, to break the mold, and adopt an innovative approach to my teaching style. Innovation leadership is about developing inner strength and clearly articulating views based on strong experience and solid judgments. Leadership in a self-renewing and thriving enterprise is characterized by a willingness to move beyond the traditional notion of merely establishing order and discipline. Instead, innovation leaders simultaneously foster experimentation and change. They encourage the generation of innovations that may not have a precedent. They know that to achieve better results, more resourcefulness is as important as more resources (Levitt, 1991). My senior learner was not afraid. He embraced change and was quietly becoming a role model for both my class and for me.

The link between the concept of innovation and higher education is such that, as education continues to grow and evolve, challenges need to be adapted to and overcome (Hesselbein, 2002). This is what is expected of our students. But, are faculty being held to the same standard and set of expectations? Hesselbein (2002) describes the importance of sharing different views and perspectives when developing an innovation such that shared understanding breeds consistent actions. This further supports the concept of requiring faculty to emulate our students by not only listening to all perspectives, but also to appreciate the complexity of their situation. The innovative approach is to listen, appreciate the situation or circumstance, and then act upon it.

Bingham (2014) builds upon this idea by proposing the concepts of innovative learning and anticipatory learning. Using forecasting techniques, simulations, scenarios, and models, anticipatory learning emphasizes learners and educators generating desirable futures and working toward these futures. Making enlightened choices from multiple future possibilities is viewed as the distinguishing characteristic of creative thinkers (Brookfield, 1987). Creativity to a certain extent can be intimidating to faculty because it tends to challenge not only their authority, but in many cases, their ability. Hence, why adopt innovations if you feel threatened? Openness and fearlessness, as a foundation of learning, should be nurtured and not discouraged in the name of intimidation (Bolman, 2008). Continuing our story, the senior learner that inspired me was a retired US Army Officer, Artillery to be exact, hence his lack of hearing, and loud booming voice. But, he was not afraid, nor was he deterred. He knew his objectives and his focus. As an innovation leader, the focus of a professor is to be what is best for each student.

Modern education mirrors business in many ways, especially regarding the roles of key stakeholders. The students can be seen as the employees. The professor can be seen as the manager/leader and is responsible for quality using a caring, purposeful manner to encourage change and contrary opinions. A professor in the role of manager/leader should encourage an exchange of ideas and nurture vitality in the classroom (DePree, 1989). Dr. Steven Sample, former President of the University of Southern California, was known for thinking outside of the box and being a true leader in and out of the classroom; he wrote a wonderful book, *The Contrarian's Guide to Leadership* that highlights many of these ideas (Sample, 2002). A gentleman that I highly respect and met at MIT, Terry Schmidt, highlighted the importance of change, constant reevaluation, and innovation in order to encourage high performance in his book entitled, *Strategic Project Management Made Simple: Practical Tools for Leaders and Teams* (Schmidt, 2009). An honest evaluation of the classroom, the student, and a self-evaluation of the professor needs to be conducted to develop successful innovations in higher education. Without this, the value of the effort will be lost and that is a loss for students. The era of the sage on the stage is long gone and today, especially with adult learners, is totally ineffective and is not well received.

Part of innovation leadership is the changing of the culture of the classroom. Culture refers to a company's values, traditions, and operating style. It is one of those vague qualities that may be, at times, difficult to measure or describe with precision, but it nevertheless exists and sets the tone for managerial and employee behavior. In a sense, the term describes how people view their workplace and how things are done (Harvard Business Essentials, 2005). The culture of the classroom is established by the professor and should be nurtured with active participation from the students. But, according to Bolman (2008) it needs to be reciprocal in nature, much like the culture of continuous innovation described earlier in this book. As in any good organization, the leadership and change needs to be initiated and modeled by the professor in the classroom.

I have been very fortunate in my career to meet some very talented individuals. In higher education, one who was memorable was Sharan Merriam, an author of over 26 books and international speaker and presenter. The concept of leading innovation is discussed in her book *Adult Learning, Linking Theory and Practice*. Merriam (2014) described innovation as a strong force in the economy that is driven by leaders that are mindful, emotionally intelligent, appreciative, and inclusive without regard to status. Over the years, many positive influences, including those I mentioned in this chapter, confirmed and reiterated what my senior learner, the retired US Army Officer, had inspired. I am confident that I am on the right path, not only for myself, but for my students as well.

Discussion

The research and personal reflections provided in this chapter have demonstrated the importance of innovation leadership in higher education. My senior learner, a retired US Army Officer, acted as the inspiration for a change and shift in my approach to higher education. The literature reviewed, ranging from admirals to highly respected academics, supports the need for innovation leadership. Innovation leadership can be applied in both K-12 and higher education. I can definitely say that I have adopted innovation leadership in my approach to teaching and that applies to my traditional classroom settings as well as my virtual, online classrooms. It has proven to be highly effective.

This story initially took place approximately eight years ago and I have found the lived experience to be rewarding, fulfilling, and challenging at times. But, most importantly, I feel it has made me a better professor and person. Not only am I able to do what I truly love, which is to teach, but I also get to learn from my students via their own lived experiences. It is a win-win situation. The challenge is following the current issues in my field. But, building solutions with my students is the fun part.

I have had the opportunity to address conferences and seminars about adult learners and their specific needs. It is an honor to do this, because this demographic is underrepresented on college campuses and online environments. Adult learners benefit from innovation leadership. I am proud to say that my senior learner graduated this past spring with his doctorate and with my prodding and encouragement, he is going to be a guest speaker at an upcoming conference focusing on adult education. The learning process never stops, nor should it, for any of us.

Summary

Clients, customers, and employees seek inspiration from leaders, but it is the duty of educators to inspire their students. Educators need to change and adapt to address their students' needs. Therefore, if an educator uses only one or two learning strategies, they may not be effective (Weisinger, 2015). Approaching each classroom experience as something new and different without the preconceived notions can build a successful learning environment. Educators and students alike need to be willing to open themselves up to new ideas and concepts in higher education.

References

Bingham, CB and Kahl, S, 2014, 'Anticipatory learning', *Strategic Entrepreneurship Journal*, vol. 8, no. 2, pp. 101–127.

Bolman, L and Deal, T, 2008, *Reframing Organizations: Artistry, Choice, and Leadership*, Jossey-Bass, San Francisco, CA.

Brookfield, S, 1987, *Developing Critical Thinkers*, Jossey-Bass, San Francisco, CA.

Brookfield, S, 1995, *Becoming a Critically Reflective Teacher*, Jossey-Bass, San Francisco, CA.

DePree, M, 1989, *Leadership Is an Art*, Dell Trade Publications, New York.

Harvard Business Essentials, 2005, *Strategy-Create and Implement the Best Strategy for Your Business*, Harvard Business School Press, Cambridge, MA.

Hesselbein, F, Goldsmith, M and Somerville, I, 2002, *Leading for Innovation*, Jossey-Bass, San Francisco, CA.

Levitt, T, 1991, *Thinking About Management*, The Free Press, New York.

Merriam, S and Bierema, L, 2014, *Adult Learning- Linking Theory and Practice*, Jossey-Bass, San Francisco, CA.

Potter, EB, 1976, *Nimitz*, Naval Institute Press, Annapolis, MD.

Sample, S and Bennis, W, 2002, *The Contrarian's Guide to Leadership*, Jossey-Bass, San Francisco, CA.

Schmidt, T, 2009, *Strategic Project Management Made Simple: Practical Tools for Leaders and Teams*, John Wiley & Sons, Hoboken, NJ.

Trulock, A, 1992, *In the Hands of Providence: Joshua L Chamberlain & The American Civil War*, The University of North Carolina Press, Chapel Hill, NC.

Weisinger, H and Pawliw-Fry, J, 2015, *Performing Under Pressure: The Science of Doing Your Best When It Matters Most*, Crown, New York, NY.

10 Sustainable community management

Norma Nusz Chandler

Sustainable communities exist due to the efforts of concerned city leaders and involved citizens. There is no one-size-fits-all solution or operating manual to guide communities when developing a sustainable initiative. This chapter will explore four elements innovation leaders should consider to help accomplish sustainable initiatives. These four elements are: destination, collaboration, evaluation, and education. There is no particular order of application of these four items as when placed into action, some or all of them may even be exercised at the same time. This chapter will review how these four elements were instrumental in Dubuque, Iowa's sustainable changes.

Innovation is critical for long term survival of an organization (Janssen, 2000; Imran, 2011). Innovative behavior is an intentional creation, introduction and application of new ideas. The method of sustainable community implementation is a new approach to encourage positive community development. Doloitte's (2013) research concluded sustainability drives innovation in a significant way. It has been determined that sustainable leaders are likely to be similar to innovation leaders. Even if an organization did not have a specific process for innovation, just including sustainability in a group's thinking process generated value (Doloitte, 2013). Thus, innovation leaders can help to drive sustainability initiatives as they provide a different perspective to analyze a situation. City leaders, as well as residents, are interested in maintaining a strong vibrant community to live in, which will be inviting to travelers and future residents.

Description

Sustainability is a new complex science harmoniously synchronizing economic, social, and ecological studies (Todorov and Marinova, 2011; Kates et al., 2001; Norgaard, 1994). The combination of these three disciplines has become known as the triple bottom line. The concept of sustainability is most often associated with the 1987 Brundtland report which described sustainability as "meeting the need of the present without comprising the needs of the future" (United Nations, 1987: para.2). Prior to the notable Brundtland report, Senator Henry Jackson in 1969 introduced a Senate bill stating the purpose of the Environmental Act was to "lay the framework for a continuing program of research and study which will ensure the present and future generations of Americans will be able to live in and enjoy an environment free of hazards to mental and physical well-being" (Luther, 2005: p. 4). Senator Jackson's bill is now known as the National Environmental Policy Act (NEPA), the first United States environmental policy. NEPA was signed by President Nixon in 1970.

The term sustainability may be relatively new, but city leaders for over a century have been interested in developing clean, heathy, productive communities. Issues discussed during the first National City Planning Conference in 1909 were similar to issues today: public health, wilderness protection, conservation of natural resources and urban parks (Daniels, 2009; Meck and Retzlaff, 2009). Cities in the progressive period, during the late 1800s to early1900s, were experiencing fast growth leading to challenges such as air-pollution from factories, sanitation issues from horse drawn transportation, water contamination from minimal sewage treatment systems, and conservation of natural resources (Daniels, 2009). Attendees of the 1909 National City Planning Conference did not speak of sustainability but rather discussed city beautification, garden cities, and conservation of natural resources. Howard (1902) published *Garden Cities of Tomorrow* in which he presented a plan to improve health, natural resources, and economics for city residents. Howard's Garden city was a combination of good attributes from country and city life while balancing development to protecting nature (Howard, 1902). Howard's intent resembles the intent of sustainability.

City leaders of today just as leaders of the past are concerned about the vibrancy of the community coupled with the health and wellbeing of the residents. Sustainable leaders are prepared to respond to a complex world (Ferdig, 2007). Traditionally, leaders focused on a particular area or discipline (Trickett and Lee, 2010). Sustainable leaders, in contrast, consider the impact on the organization by all three elements of the triple bottom line: profit, people and the planet (Tideman, Arts and Zandeem, 2013; Quinn and Baltes, 2007). Newtonian physics and Darwinian biology place humans as the superior survivors above the natural environment, economy, and social elements, but now organizations consider themselves as a non-autonomous part; inseparable from the social, economic, and natural environment. Long term survival of organizations will require strong leaders who recognize interdependence with stakeholders and the ecological systems; possess exceptional moral courage; and are open minded long range planners (Mackey, 2007; Tideman, Arts and Zandeem, 2013).

Siciliano (2012) explained leadership as a process of influencing people; leaders must not harm their followers but motivate the entire organization in healthy productive endeavors. Sustainable leaders do not have to have a formal leadership role in a city rather they can be regular citizens striving to take account for their impact on the local and global environment, society and economics (Ferdig, 2007). Ferdig explained sustainable leaders operate on an expanded view of how the complex universe operates which includes realizing paradox, contradictions, and view point differences are natural characteristics of healthy human network interaction. Though it can be challenging to contend with conflict while working with different viewpoints, sustainable leaders must be able to put their egos aside and consider the many perspectives of a situation and allow concepts to meld together for a rewarding result. Sharing knowledge and insight is characteristic of sustainable leaders. Both good and bad is to be shared as it allows others to learn from their mistakes and make improvements to success (Ferdig, 2007; Ferdig and Ludema, 2005).

Leaders must realize actions in one area of an organization may have adverse implications in other areas (Ferdig, 2007). No single action is isolated, but is intrinsically linked with other results. While traditional leadership skills; strategic thinking, contingency planning, communicating, and coordinating remain critical, the sustainable leader engages other leaders to make a sustainable impact on the organization and community (Ferdig, 2007). Adverse repercussions can be reduced when leaders from different areas with similar desires collaborate, explore, learn, and devise a realistic course of action (Ferdig, 2007). Sustainable leadership requires a holistic approach where everything is connected.

The story

Cities around the world are addressing sustainability in different ways and for various reasons. Dubuque, Iowa will be briefly reviewed in part because of the city's success in implementing sustainable practices but as an example of how it utilized innovative approaches to achieve sustainable goals. Dubuque's successful history reveals four elements of sustainable leadership were utilized repeatedly. These four sustainable leadership elements: destination, collaboration, evaluation, and education may be applied repeatedly and in different orders as will be seen in the following case study.

Dubuque, Iowa, is a progressive community located in eastern Iowa on the Mississippi River with a population of approximately 58,000 people. Dubuque was not always a vibrant city. In the 1980s, it led the United States in unemployment (23 percent) which was attributed to the Midwest farm crisis and collapse of local manufacturing (Knight Foundation, 2013). The city of Dubuque set sustainability as a priority goal in 2006 when Mayor Roy D. Buol received full City Council support to focus on sustainability. Dubuque began its sustainable transformation by involving individuals from the city and surrounding community. The City Council approval to create a city-wide taskforce which included individuals with diverse backgrounds: local government, schools, utility companies, religious organizations, neighborhood associations, youth groups, non-profits, environmental organizations and business leaders. Nearly 900 community surveys were completed to gain insight on citizens' needs and desires. Dubuque 2.0, a community engagement initiative, was started in 2009 by the Community Foundation of Greater Dubuque and

Dubuque Area Chamber of Commerce. Dubuque 2.0 represents over 1,400 businesses and 400 non-profits to inspire sustainability throughout the community, implementing projects like the Sustainability Challenge, community cafes, and a Green Asset Map. The Dubuque 2.0 Foundation identified what they called the missing link: awareness and participation of individual residents. The foundation joined forces with City Hall's Sustain Dubuque and area businesses such as IBM (Knight Foundation, 2013). Many different approaches were utilized to engage citizens and learn directly from individuals about what was working and their recommended changes. Some of the engagement activities include: community cafés, resident surveys, personal resource use, online and offline community games. Community cafés held in participating restaurants provided residents an opportunity to discuss sustainable issues. Generally 30–50 people attended events resulting in greater understanding and regulation change support. Surveys assisted in identifying community priorities, and gaps in resources and services. Personalized resource use data, a pilot program, allowed users to compare their water and electrical use. Online and offline community games encouraged action in learning, in contrast to passive observation. Participants learned ways to reduce their carbon and water footprints. Cash prizes and a point system provided incentive for behavior changes (Knight Foundation, 2013). These are just a few tools Dubuque has utilized to educate community members.

The Dubuque Sustainable Initiative raised awareness about the importance of measuring community sustainability. In 2011, the City of Dubuque determined that a single model was not sufficient and partnered with the University of Iowa School of Urban and Regional Planning. This partnership stimulated the development of 60 qualitative and quantitative indicators relating to 11 principle areas of sustainability. Their indicators did not provide a firm rating of a community's sustainability. Rather the data reported Dubuque's historical trend and how it correlated to selected comparison cities. The indicator project provided insight on what was going well in the community and potential areas to focus on for the future. Concluding remarks in Dubuque's Sustainability Progress Report 2012 state that goals should be set and regular data updates should be completed to more effectively monitor changes.

In 2014, Dubuque joined the STAR Community network and began collecting more data. On April 2, 2015 a 4-STAR rating was achieved. Due to the dynamics of the data, the STAR Community Rating lasts for three years after the award date. Ratings range from 1 to 5-STAR with a 5-STAR being the highest rating. Participating communities may select measures from a list on which to report data, therefore it is not a true head-to-head comparison as each community could have a different combination of indicators. It is a rating not a ranking system (STAR Communities, 2016).

The City of Dubuque shares best practices with other cities and initiated a sustainable conference called Growing Sustainable Communities in 2005. The conference hosts national and global speakers for public- and private-sector leaders with an interest in sustainability. Dubuque is also a participant in the

Urban Sustainability Directors Network (USDN) Heartland Local Government Sustainability Network. USDN (2016) allows local government sustainable professionals from the United States and Canada to share best practices and to promote urban solutions. Plastric and Parzen (2012) explained a typical reason for establishing a network is peer-to-peer exchange and learning. Peer learning is an initial step to pursuing more difficult tasks such as inventing solutions and influencing state and federal policy makers (Plastric and Parzen, 2012). Sustainable insight is also passed on to other communities through published documents, web sites, conferences, networking and conversation.

Sustainable Dubuque is a community-created, citizen-led initiative. Under the 2006 umbrella initiative which set sustainability as a priority Dubuque developed goals and objectives. Indicator data has been collected and evaluated to help monitor and guide future projects. Success is attributed to Dubuque's balanced long-term life quality approach where no one in the community is left out. Dubuque's sustainability commitment has led to greater awareness "that our community is like an ecosystem, where everything is truly linked to everything" (Carstens, 2010: 11). The City of Dubuque is continually expanding awareness, creating partnerships and encouraging community involvement (Sustainable Dubuque, 2012).

Discussion

Today's sustainable leaders recognize, as Howard did in his 1902 Garden City Plan, the importance of addressing the three areas of economics, culture, and environment for the development of a vibrant city which would improve the quality of life for people and help maintain the resources for future generations. Since it is difficult for one individual to possess all of this knowledge, communities should consider utilizing a sustainable leadership team to orchestrate environmental community development. Sixteen of Chicago's City Center of Sustainability managers felt having diverse skills in their organization brought broader solution opportunities for projects (Young, 2010). The Chicago city managers realized the value of multi-disciplinary working together as did city leaders in Dubuque, IA. The City of Dubuque developed a comprehensive plan that integrated the three pillars of sustainability. Dubuque's use of the sustainability pillars along with a multi-disciplinary focused task force, transformed its community into a leader of sustainability.

The characteristics of sustainable leadership which will be discussed below align with Ferdig's (2007) thoughts about what sustainable leaders can do to be more successful: collaborate, explore, learn, and devise a realistic course of action. The order of the four items is not indicative of a step process or priority of importance as sustainable leaders apply these four items continually and sometimes all at the same time through a planning process. The four critical elements of developing a strong healthy community where people want to live are:

- Destination/goal
- Collaboration
- Evaluation/measure
- Education/share

Destination/goal: More is accomplished when organizations have established goals. Leaders have defined a direction of what needs to be accomplished next and what the organization is to accomplish. Mapes and Wolch (2011) explained the breadth and depth of a sustainable community was due to the goals and outcome. Establishment of goals allowed communities to impact not only neighborhoods but individuals. In some situations the sustainable initiative impact can go beyond the city. Sustainability generally does not just happen; it needs a plan to provide guidance. Adger and Jordan (2009) explain a direction needs to be carefully thought through and deliberated over prior to execution. Sustainable progress should satisfy all partners (Esty and Winston, 2009). Establishing a target allows not only the sustainability committee but the whole city administration and city residents to recognize the goal and align themselves to help achieve desired results.

Dawn Rittenhouse, DuPont's Director of Sustainable Development, explained that setting seemingly impossible goals, like zero or beyond zero, encourages strategic thinking and transformation in the organization. Stretch goals may not be met immediately but in the long run more is accomplished (Tebo, 2015; Esty and Winston, 2009). Setting what may seem like an impossible stretch goal may be an extreme approach, but it goes along with the thought more is accomplished if a goal has been determined. Establishing a direction allows much more to be achieved. Caution should be exercised when setting goals so that they are not too extreme as the goals should never overextend the organization's ability. Esty and Winston (2009) expressed that once the goal is publicized, it is no longer voluntary. Stakeholders will be expecting change and may be disappointed if they do not see progress.

Collaboration: Sustainable leaders have been realizing that everything is connected (Carstens, 2010; Ferdig, 2005). Complex interconnectivity of sustainable issues lends itself to system thinking (Hunting and Tilbury, 2006). Traditional analysis separates an individual element. Jay Forrester (1998), the father of system thinking, explained systems dynamics in contrast to traditional analysis as a dynamic complex process which considers the impact the single element has on the various parts of the whole system (Aronson, 1996; León, 2008; Trombulak, 2016). There is no end to the systems as the systems thinking process attempts to review the impact the single element has on each aspect of a system. It is a very comprehensive look at relationships between various components in an organization. Systems thinking is a rather big concept when a person pauses to consider their implications. Everything is interconnected and it could be impossible to assess the interconnectedness of a situation (Senge, n.d.). Sustainable leaders, when developing plans, should work with and consider as many stakeholders as practical.

Sustainable partnerships will require leaders to breakdown traditional silos/compartments between interdisciplinary strategies, departments, and government agencies. Benton-Short and Cseh (2015) explain that sustainable community plans include key leaders from various municipal departments such as parks and recreation, engineering, zoning, sanitation, and many others. Local community organizations and non-profit groups can assist municipalities gain public input by way of community meetings and workshops; this was undertaken in the development of extensive plans (Benton-Short and Cseh, 2015). Strong working relationships are needed between industry, government, and non-profit and general public. The United States government has led by example. On June 16, 2009 EPA, HUD and DOT joined to improve access to affordable housing, provide more transportation options, and lower transportation costs while protecting the environment (EPA, 2010). Positive communication between groups can help assure all relevant resources are being utilized. Coordination between groups can also help minimize cost, reduce redundancy, and minimize conflict (EPA, 2016). People in every aspect of a project need to work together as the project could include multiple departments which in the traditional work structure have been isolated from each other. It could mean different government agencies such as city, township, county, and state would need to work together to minimize an adverse impact on citizens.

Tideman, Arts, and Zandee (2013) point out that the values of business, the economy, the environment, and society are no longer separate. This requires leaders to modify their traditional problem solving approaches. A dynamic process described by Porter and Kramer (2006, 2011) as 'creating shared value' allows the stakeholder's economic and social values to be considered to develop new opportunities. Social values cover a range of areas similar to sustainability: environmental impact, energy use, health, and safety just to mention a few. Businesses such as GE, Google, IBM, Intel, Johnson and Johnson, Nestlé, Unilever, and Walmart have experienced profit by requiring their leaders to develop a deeper appreciation for societal needs and to collaborate across profit/non-profit boundaries. Internal and external municipal collaborations will lead to more successful sustainable plans in part due to the comprehensive input but also each party will be able to educate others about how issues can impact different entities (Benton-Short and Cseh, 2015).

The sustainable leader's role in working with multiple departments and disciplines inside and outside the community offices is just as critical for the success of the environmental project as influencing the local citizens (Bossink, 2007). These leaders should be strategic thinkers with exceptional moral courage who can withstand scrutiny and criticism while being instrumental in establishing long term goals and procedures. Senge et al. (2008) explained that collaboration is about relationships that demonstrate genuine caring and mutual vulnerability. The three capabilities of collaboration, convening, listening, and nurturing a shared commitment, are not always easy to accomplish. Hard work and the best of people are needed as participants to work between departments and or organizations.

Measure: A method of bringing understanding to a complex system is through the use of several measurements or indicators. Meadows (1998) explained indicators as means of measuring and monitoring things people care about and value. Developing indicators and monitoring change will help assist people to better understand a city's intent (Mapes and Wolch, 2011; Johnson and Schaltegger, 2016). The complex nature of sustainability measuring or monitoring a community's sustainability can be an extremely complex enduring process but a very important element of success.

Sustainable communities develop due to many items; this makes it difficult to limit what is measured. Sustainable indicators can never capture the full picture of a community's sustainable efforts (Burbach, 2012). They can, however, help define key aspects of specific items (Pinter et al., 2005). Several models/methods of monitoring a community's sustainable practices are being utilized, but there is not a definitive recognized standard with the possible exception of Sustainability Tools for Assessing and Rating Communities (STAR Communities). STAR Communities, the first voluntary framework for evaluating liveability and sustainability of United States communities, was released in October 2012 (STAR Communities, 2013).

Indicator systems are comprised of quantitative and qualitative indices, which should address all three global systems: humanity, economy, and nature (Scerri and James, 2010). A sustainable model should assess one component against the other two components such as economy against humanity and nature. Sustainable development should synchronize and harmonize the economic, social, and ecological processes while remaining separate from the political sustainability development process (Todorov and Marinova, 2011; Pinter et al., 2005). Todorov and Marinova (2011) explain a sustainable global development system as a meta-system which is in a state of dynamic balance. The system is in a state of equilibrium which does not cause vibration/fluctuation. Indicator models should provide decision makers relevant, unbiased, and scientific evidence (Pinter et al., 2005; Hasna, 2009).

Various types of indicator models: (a) quantitative, (b) physical, (c) conceptual, and (d) standardized are available but can never capture the full sustainable story of a community (Todorov and Marinova, 2011; Burbach, 2012; Kline, 2000). As an example, an indicator may address the number of acres of wetlands that were lost but it does not investigate if wetlands lost were essential for (a) flood control, (b) wildlife habitat, or (c) city development (Kline, 2000). However, indicators have been known to promote interactive knowledge sharing, which in turn has led to building relationships enabling citizens to learn from each other. Mutual sharing of knowledge results in improving understanding and practices on a given sector of the community (Gonzalez et al., 2011). People who share knowledge/information share their values and allow communities to better evaluate situations and make better informed decisions which are more agreeable to all parties and will have a more positive result (Kline, 2000; Meadows, 1998). Sustainable indicators provide a solid basis for all levels of community decision-making and help communities be self-regulating if indicators are integrated with environmental and development systems (Ghosh et al., 2006; Meadows, 1998). Indicators have been a critical tool, helping people gain more control over their lives and ensure a healthier future for themselves and the next generation (Kline, 2000; Hasna, 2009; Yigitcanlar and Dur, 2009).

Share/educate: The science of sustainability is a relatively new concept. Sustainable community leaders will need to educate people from the city administration to the residents. Some people are completely unfamiliar with the term sustainability. Some recognize the concept by a different term while others believe it only relates to recycling household waste or using less fuel. It is therefore important to reinforce an understanding of sustainability as a complex system. Learning about sustainable communities involves under-standing an interdependent and balanced relationship between society, culture, politics, and economics. Educators should focus on conveying the intent of sustainable practices, knowledge-sharing, and renewal. Sharing best practices with other communities and helping them learn from each other's experiences will promote more improvement. Educating people about complex sustainable principles will allow them to understand the importance of engaging in sustainable practices. This continual educational process could be viewed as an extended appreciative inquiry process. Appreciative inquiry theory is, as explained by Cooperrider and Whitney (n.d.), an affirmative process where the union between people and the orga-nization that they discuss comes together for a positive outcome. The group is able to analyze each of the multiple ideas then combine them for positive outcome which does not inversely impact anyone. The whole process builds knowledge and energy for the community and all other communities which learn from each other.

Sharing knowledge with other communities is important as it allows all parties to expand and improve. A partnership for Sustainable Cities was an idea during a 2009 meeting which developed into a firm commitment (Hoornweg and Freire, 2013). Seattle is a city known for implementing better sustainable policies which have helped to promote competiveness, attract business and deal with pollution, and so is known as a good learning city. Since 1993, Seattle has been cultivating relationships with cities to capture best practices.

One benefit from collaborating with multiple entities when working on a sustainable community project is the ability to gain knowledge. Businesses like IBM, Cisco Systems, and Philips have partnered with local communities by concentrating on particular areas of sustainability. For example, Philips' Livable Cities Program focuses on how lighting can influence the quality of life, improve public safety, increase energy efficiency, and enhance mental health (Hoornweg and Freire, 2013). A critical role of sustainable leadership is to influence community citizens to be involved, committed and even take ownership of the project (Carstens, 2010).

Summary

Whatever the organization, there is a desire for leadership competencies to achieve superior organizational performance (Quinn and Baltes, 2007). Dubuque city leaders had a desire to improve their community for the residents. This realization prompted the utilization of innovation leadership to promote change and achieve a sustainable community. A community where residents would have economic security, a better quality of life and healthy ecosystems for many years into the future.

Four elements used for innovative sustainable development discussed in this chapter were: destination, collaboration, evaluation and education. Similarities can be seen in these four elements and the CREATE Model explained earlier in the book. Destination is setting a goal. Establishing a city sustainable goal helps the city departments focus on incorporating sustainable practices in their activities. A city goal also encourages all community organizations and individuals to concentrate their efforts. The complex nature of sustainability links multiple community entities together. Communities are like eco-systems (Carstens, 2019), making it critical that all stakeholders work together. Actions taken by one group can affect the whole community. Collection of solid data provides leaders the ability to make decisions based on sound information rather than perception. Leaders are able to evaluate data to identify priorities and monitor change. The last element addressed in this chapter was education. Sharing sustainable information within a community is as critical as passing it on to other cities. Reinforcing peoples' understanding of the complexity of sustainability allows them to be more engaged resulting in a more positive impact.

Sustainability is not a rocket science but is a new science that intertwines humanity with old and new technologies (Scerri and James, 2010). Many tools are available which can assist sustainable development in a community, however at the base of each sustainable plan are four elements: destination, collaboration, evaluation, and education. These four items are always in play in a dynamic sustainable plan. A natural instinct is to always make improvements: in the case of a sustainable community there is desire to make innovative changes based on the triple bottom line resulting in improving the quality of life for all.

References

Adger, N and Jordan, A, 2009, *Governing Sustainability*. Cambridge University Press, New York.

Aronson, D, 1996, *Overview of Systems Thinking*. Available at http://wwwthinkingnet/Systems_Thinking/OverviewSTarticlepdf [Accessed 25 Aug. 2017].

Bossink, BAG, 2007, 'Leadership for sustainable innovation', *International Journal of Technology Management & Sustainable Development*, vol. 6, no. 2, pp. 135–149.

Benton-Short, L, and Cseh, M, 2015, 'Changing cities, changing culture', *Advances In Developing Human Resources*, vol. 17, no. 4, pp. 460–472.

Burbach, C, 2012, *Creating the Sustainable City: A Community Engagement Strategy that's Working*. Available at http://mcgraw-hillresearchfoundationorg/wp-content/uploads/2012/09/Dubuque-paper-09_27_12-FINALSPpdf [Accessed 25 Aug. 2017].

98 *Norma Nusz Chandler*

Carstens, L, 2010, 'Defining, inspiring, and implementing sustainability', *National Civic Review*, vol. 99, no. 3, pp. 11–16.
Cooperrider, D and Whitney, D, n.d., *A Positive Revolution in Change: Appreciative Inquiry*. Available at https://appreciativeinquirycaseedu/uploads/Whatisai.pdf [Accessed 25 Aug. 2017].
Daniels, TL, 2009, 'A trail across time: American environmental planning from city beautiful to sustainability', *Journal of the American Planning Association*, vol. 75, no. 2, pp. 178–192.
Doloitte, 2013, 'Sustainability Driven Innovation: Harnessing sustainability's ability to spark innovation'. Available at http://wwwgreenproforg/wp-content/uploads/2013/12/Sustainability_Driven_Innovation_102513pdf [Accessed 25 Aug. 2017].
EPA, 2010, 'Partnership for sustainable communities: A year of progress for American communities'. Available at https://nepisepagov/Exe/ZyNETexe/P1008O9Dtxt?ZyActionD=ZyDocument&Client=EPA&Index=2006%20Thru%202010&Docs=&Query=&Time=&EndTime=&SearchMethod=1&TocRestrict=n&Toc=&TocEntry=&QField=&QFieldYear=&QFieldMonth=&QFieldDay=&UseQField=&IntQFieldOp=0&ExtQFieldOp=0&XmlQuery=&File=D%3A%5CZYFILES%5CINDEX%20DATA%5C06THRU10%5CTXT%5C00000021%5CP1008O9Dtxt&User=ANONYMOUS&Password=anonymous&SortMethod=h%7C-&MaximumDocuments=1&FuzzyDegree=0&ImageQuality=r75g8/r75g8/x150y150g16/i425&Display=p%7Cf&DefSeekPage=x&SearchBack=ZyActionL&Back=ZyActionS&BackDesc=Results%20page&MaximumPages=1&ZyEntry=1&SeekPage=x [Accessed 25 Aug. 2017].
EPA, 2016, 'Framework for creating a smart growth economic development strategy: a tool for small cities and towns'. Available at https://wwwepagov/sites/production/files/2016–01/documents/small_town_econ_dev_tool_010516.pdf [Accessed 25 Aug. 2017].
Esty, DC and Winston, AS, 2009, *Green to Gold: How Smart Companies Use Environmental Strategy to Innovate, Create Value, and Build Competitive Advantage*. John Wiley and Sons, Hoboken, NJ.
Ferdig, MA, 2007, 'Sustainability Leadership: Co-creating a sustainable future', *Journal of Change Management*, vol. 7, no. 1, pp. 25–35.
Ferdig, MA and Ludema, JD, 2005, *Transformative Interactions: Qualities of Conversation that Heighten the Vitality of Self-Organizational Change*. Available at http://wwwsustainabilityleadershipinstituteorg/downloads/Ferdig_CH05.PDF [Accessed 25 Aug. 2017].
Forrester, JW, 1989, *The Beginning of System Dynamics*. Available at http://webmitedu/sysdyn/sd-intro/D-4165-1.pdf [Accessed 25 Aug. 2017].
Ghosh, S, Vale, R and Vale, B, 2006, 'Indications from Sustainability Indicators', *Journal of Urban Design*, vol. 11, no. 2, pp. 263–275.
Gonzalez, A, Donnelly, A, Jones, M, Klostermann, J, Groot, A and Breil, M, 2011, 'Community of practice approach to developing urban sustainability indicators', *Journal of Environmental Assessment Policy & Management*, vol. 13, no. 4, pp. 591–617.
Hasna, AM, 2009, 'Ethics and sustainability in engineering'. Available at http://wwwinter-disciplinarynet/wp-content/uploads/2009/06/Hasna-Paper1.pdf [Accessed 25 Aug. 2017].
Hoornweg, D and Freire, M, 2013, *Building Sustainability in an Urbanizing World*. Washington, DC.
Howard, E, 1902, *Garden City of Tomorrow*. Available at http://wwwlibrarycornelledu/Reps/DOCS/howard.htm [Accessed 25 Aug. 2017].

Hunting, SA and Tilbury, D, 2006, 'Shifting towards sustainability: Six insights into successful organizational change for sustainability', Australian Research Institute in Education for Sustainability, ARIES, Sydney.

Imran, R and Anis-ul-Haque, M, 2011, 'Mediating effect of organizational climate between transformational leadership and innovative work behavior', *Pakistan Journal of Psychological Research*, vol. 26, no. 2, pp. 183–199.

Janssen, O, 2000, 'Job demands, perceptions of effort–reward fairness and innovative work behaviour', *Journal of Occupational & Organizational Psychology*, vol. 73, no. 3, pp. 287–302.

Johnson, MP and Schaltegger, S, 2016, 'Two decades of sustainability management tools for SMEs: How far have we come?', *Journal of Small Business Management*, vol. 54, no. 2 pp. 481–505.

Kates, RW, Clark, WC, Corell, R, Hall, JM, Jaeger, CC, Lowe, I and Mooney, H, 2001, 'Sustainability science', *Science*, vol. 292, no. 5517, p. 641.

Kline, E, 2000, 'Planning and creating eco-cities: indicators as a tool for shaping development and measuring', *Local Environment*, vol. 5, no. 3, p. 343.

Knight Foundation, 2013, 'Dubuque 20: How the community foundation of greater Dubuque used environmental information to spark citizen action'. Available at http://icmaorg/en/icma/knowledge_network/documents/kn/Document/304684/Dubuque_ 20_How_the_Community_Foundation_of_Greater_Dubuque_Used_Environmental_ Information_to_Spark_C [Accessed 25 Aug. 2017].

León, JA, 2008, 'Systems thinking: the key for the creation of truly desired futures', *International Journal of Reality Therapy*, vol. 28, no. 1, pp. 15–20.

Luther, L, 2005, 'The national environmental policy act: Background and implementation', *RL33152 Congressional Research Service: Report*, 1–38. Available at http://wwwftadotgov/documents/Unit1_01CRSReport.pdf [Accessed 25 Aug. 2017].

Mackey, J, 2007, 'Conscious capitalism: Creating a new paradigm for business'. Available at http://wwwwholeplanetfoundationorg/files/uploaded/John_Mackey-Conscious_Capitalism.pdf [Accessed 25 Aug. 2017].

Mapes, J and Wolch, J, 2011, 'Living green: The promise and pitfalls of new sustainable communities', *Journal of Urban Design*, vol. 16, no. 1, pp. 105–126.

Meadows, D, 1998, 'Indicators and information systems for sustainable development Balton Group'. Available at http://wwwsustainabilityinstituteorg/pubs/Indicators& Information.pdf [Accessed 25 Aug. 2017].

Meck, S and Retzlaff, RC, 2009, 'A familiar ring: A retrospective on the first national conference on city planning 1909', *Planning & Environmental Law*, vol. 61, no. 4, pp. 3–10.

Meck, S and Retzlaff, RC, 2012, 'President Jimmy Carter's urban policy: A reconstruction and an appraisal', *Journal of Planning History*, vol. 11, no. 3, pp. 242–280.

Norgaard, R, 1994, *Development Betrayed: Then End of the Progress and a Coevolutionary Revisioning of the Future*, Routledge Chapman & Hall, New York.

Pinter, L, Hardi, P and Bartelmus, P, 2005, 'Indicators of sustainable development: proposals for a way forward'. Available at http://wwwiisdorg/pdf/2005/measure_ indicators_sd_way_forward.pdf [Accessed 25 Aug. 2017].

Plastrik, P and Parzen, J, 2012, *Urban Sustainability Directors Network, USDN, Regional Network Development Guidebook*. Available at http://usdnorg/uploads/cms/ documents/usdn-regional-network-development-guidebook.pdf [Accessed 25 Aug. 2017].

Porter, ME and Kramer, MR, 2006, 'Strategy & society: the link between competitive advantage and corporate social responsibility', *Harvard Business Review*, vol. 84, no. 2, pp. 78–92.

Porter, ME and Kramer, MR, 2011, 'Creating shared value', *Harvard Business Review*, vol. 89, no. 1, pp. 62–77.

Scerri, A and James, P, 2010, 'Accounting for sustainability: Combining qualitative and quantitative research in developing indicators of sustainability', *International Journal of Social Research Methodology*, vol. 13, no. 1, pp. 41–53.

Senge, P, (n.d.), *Systems Thinking.* Available at https://wwwsolonlineorg/?page=Systems Thinking [Accessed 25 Aug. 2017].

Senge, P, Kruschwitz, K, Laur, J and Schley, S, 2008, *The Necessary Revolution: Working Together to Create a Sustainable World*, Broadway Books: New York.

Siciliano, V, 2012, 'Leadership beyond the triple bottom line', *Sustainable Industries.* Available at http://sustainableindustriescom/articles/2012/03/leadership-beyond-triple-bottom-line [Accessed 25 Aug. 2017].

STAR Communities, 2013, 'History & development'. Available at http://wwwsta rcommunitiesorg/rating-system/history [Accessed 25 Aug. 2017].

STAR Communities, 2016, 'Dubuque, IA recognized for sustainability excellence'. Available at http://wwwstarcommunitiesorg/press-releases/dubuque-ia-recognized-for-sustainability-excellence/ [Accessed 25 Aug. 2017].

Sustainable Dubuque, 2012, 'Creating a national model for sustainability'. Available at http://wwwcityofdubuqueorg/DocumentCenter/Home/View/2702 [Accessed 25 Aug. 2017].

Tebo, P, 2015, 'Sustainable Scotland network annual conference'. Available at https://wwwyoutubecom/watch?v=9q0mAjxnOtA [Accessed 25 Aug. 2017].

Tideman, SG, Arts, MC and Zandee, DP, 2013, 'Sustainable Leadership', *Journal of Corporate Citizenship*, vol. 49, pp. 17–33.

Todorov, V and Marinova, D, 2011, 'Modelling Sustainability', *Mathematics and Computers in Simulation*, vol. 81, no. 7, pp. 1397–1408.

Trickett, L and Lee, P, 2010, 'Leadership of subregional places in the context of growth', *Policy Studies*, vol. 31, no. 4, pp. 429–440.

Trombulak, S, 2016, 'Jay Forrester, the father of systems thinking'. Available at http://sitesmiddleburyedu/schooloftheenvironment/category/systems-thinking/ [Accessed 25 Aug. 2017].

Quinn, L and Baltes, J, 2007, 'Leadership and the triple bottom line'. Available at http s://www.ccl.org/leadership/pdf/research/tripleBottomLine.pdf [Accessed 25 Aug. 2017].

United Nations, 1987, 'Report of the World Commission on Environment And Development'. Accessed at http://wwwunorg/documents/ga/res/42/ares42-187.htm [Accessed 25 Aug. 2017].

USDN, 2016, 'Connecting people fostering innovation'. Available at http://usdnorg/homehtml?returnUrl=%2findex.html [Accessed 25 Aug. 2017].

Yigitcanlar, T and Dur, F, 2009, 'Developing a sustainability assessment model: the sustainable infrastructure, land-use, environment and transport model of sustainability'. Available at http://eprintsquteduau/38638/ [Accessed 25 Aug. 2017].

Young, RF, 2010, 'The greening of Chicago: Environmental leaders and organizational learning in the transition toward a sustainable metropolitan region', *Journal of Environmental Planning and Management*, vol. 53, no. 8, pp. 1051–1068.

11 Working well with cultures in the Middle East

Ward E. Marshall

Innovation leadership often requires building bridges to span a cultural divide. As the world becomes more global, cultural awareness is required in order to influence others and bring us closer together. Cross-cultural engagement means dealing with possibilities and probabilities rather than certainties. While many societies have a relatively defined culture, the behavior of individuals is not entirely predictable, nor is it without moral, ethical, and cultural restrictions within a level of expectable norms, trends, and patterns. Societies shape and influence the core values and ethics of individuals to various degrees. Innovation leadership requires the intuitive identification of behavioral patterns and influences that prevail at the time, sub-culture, and location. Islam remains the major moral and cultural foundation and code of ethics in the Middle East.

Description

With the advent of mass Arab media, such as Al-Jazeera, many dialects of Arabic have faded and are trending toward a singular, but not social unity. The Arab culture has a predominant mindset focused on collectivism rather than individualism. While simplicity and commonality are used to explain a complex society and its leadership requirements, one would be foolhardy to stereotype or over-simplify cultural differences and the difficulty in overcoming or accommodating challenges. Most of a society will follow a social norm but individuals exist that influence their dynamic segment of society. The culture is stratified and position and status are extremely important. Arab culture remains fractious yet shares some degree of unanimity (Elbadawi, 2010).

Leadership in this dynamic culture is a deductive process that requires situational and cultural awareness, information gathering, and common sense interpretation to develop logical answers to leadership challenges within the complex context. Mental flexibility is required to perceive, think, and consider the perspective of a vastly different culture. The interpretation of a cultural response to make sense of a situation requires an understanding of that culture at an intuitive level. A leader must determine what can be done, what should be done, and what cannot be done within the cultural framework.

Tacit knowledge of a culture and its variations leads to situational awareness and perspective that is useful in evaluating a situation and influencing others through adaptive leadership (Al-Omari, 2008). The knowledge of commonalities and variations in regional religion, values, aspirations, frustrations, and history generate situational awareness and guides the actions of the innovation leader. The holistic consideration of another's perspective can position a leader for meaningful advancement in achieving goals and objectives beyond one's own culture and ambitions. Mutual objectives and common consensus while bestowing honor, status, and respect on the decision maker is a method of advancing goals as a leader.

The story

As I entered Afghanistan, a region with a vastly different culture, it was obvious that there was a great divide between my culture and Afghans. Even among villages, towns and camps of Afghans, there was immeasurable difference of perspective and cultural rift. There were defining tribal confederations and regional alignments as well as religious branching. Few that live in Afghanistan identify themselves as Afghan, instead, they identify with culture, religion, region, and family. The prevalent tribalism that remains in Afghanistan after millennia of the close living relationship was amazing. While being a loosely associated group from a common geological area, Afghans also had very strong internal ties and loyalties. The old adage: me against my brother, my brother and I against my uncle, and all of us against the foreigner, held some truth.

Rudyard Kipping, in *The Ballad of East and West* in 1895, wrote about his time in Afghanistan: "East is the East and the West is the West and never the twain shall meet." At first, I was unaware of the vast cultural gap and did not know that I was going into a traditionally collective culture with deeply held values and beliefs different from my individualist culture. The Afghan culture remains diverse within it and is a fractious poly ethnic group for both inside and outside perspectives. Yet, they shared what they had with my small team and grew to accept us. Some of my closest relationships were built with people that I previously had little in common with.

What I had taken for granted as ethics and values were challenged. This high context culture was one that used collectivism to save face. The culture uses a complex and sophisticated communication system with a predisposition for implicit rather than explicit communication. My first encounters were in controlled environments where my culture was prevalent, but it was obvious that as time progressed that my exposure to new ideas, language, and culture would change my perspective and ideas, such as exchanging urgency for timing and diplomacy. Hospitality was never an option; it was required for any meaningful or purposeful discussion. Afghan cultures offered a stark contrast to western culture; the different fractured cultures were distinctly divided and characterized various villages. When meeting with the elders in an Afghan village for a Jirga, one must remember that time is abundant in Afghanistan; time for hospitality, meeting time, time for discussion, plenty of time to consider, thus a leader must display an abundance of patience. My time as an Advisor to Afghan security forces was a unique preparation for understanding experiences in Iraq.

The culture of Iraq was widely divided on religious fragmentation with loyalty to family and perhaps the tribe or tribal confederation (Polk, 2006). Understanding and identifying rifts were paramount to achieving a better relationship and progress toward mutually beneficial accomplishments. Iraqis identified as Sunni or Shiite and in part as Arab, Persian, or Kurd, rather than by family or clan. An effective leader is required to be aware of division and understand why there is a difference, its meaning and effect on perspective, and hence, decisions and actions. An innovation leader will bridge the differences, build efficacious solutions to persistent problems, and produce relationships to advance the interests of all parties involved.

When I volunteered for the assignment in Iraq, I spent some time selecting from open positions, of which, I selected Deputy Director of Interagency Coordination. However, the position I was coopted to fill was Advisor to the Iraqi Ground Forces, Commander, Commander of a Mobile Training Team, and the management of a translator and linguist pool. The team was functionally aligned at the national level between United States Ground Forces Command and Iraq Ground Forces. I was initially disappointed in the selection, as Advisor positions are perceived as dangerous. However, time would prove that the selection was in the best interest of everyone involved. I had no time to prepare for Iraqi cultural nuances. Therefore, I started reading books such as *Understanding Iraq* and *Understanding Iran* by William R. Polk and rereading the *Shia Revival* by Vali Nasr. My previous experience had been as an Advisor to Afghan Security Forces and the International Stabilization Force Afghanistan. Mentally, I needed to prepare myself for a cultural adaptation to gain trust and build mutual respect within diverse cultures and subcultures of Iraq. The appreciation for varied culture and perspective is a great asset in the facilitation of mutual understanding through patient and thoughtful communication. What often seems like a single homogenous culture is often a conglomeration of diverse subcultures and symbiotic and sometimes ancillary cultures working together in an orchestrated collective society as described by Dr. Jehad Al-Omari in his book *Understanding the Arab Culture*. Intellectual awareness generates meaningful situational awareness and sensitivity to cultural cues. Keen observation and situational awareness are required to gain a meaningful understanding of the circumstances and interrelationships of a dynamic society. As one is unable to gather complete information on the dynamics of a new culture, initial leadership is more a situation of general observations on a macro scale with some nuances key to anticipating change and response.

Middle Eastern society is a high context culture with a culture of collective decision-making. The unifying elements of the Arab culture include a language that is shared within a religion. Since leadership is the art of influencing others, a profound vicarious empathy toward this fractural culture is required in order to generate a dispassionate perspective and understanding that is a meaningful situational interpretation. The culture is held together by a common macro religion and separated by ideology, interpretation of cultural nuance, regional affiliation, and ethnic background. Intuitive leadership is difficult in such a vivacious environment that has a much different cultural context.

The basis for understanding leadership is developed during the important task of identifying the competencies and meta-competencies that comprise leadership and more specifically situational leadership. For this discussion, we will use the seven meta-competencies provided to us by Tubbs (2006). Tubbs provides a discussion matrix about leadership that includes: understanding the big picture, teamwork and followership, attitude, leadership, communication, innovative and creative thought, leading change. In addition to the Tubbs meta-competencies, we will consider Middle Eastern cultural complexity in conjunction with the influence of leadership (Bates, 2001). The most notable cultural difference in the region is the division between Sunni and Shiite as outlined by Vali Nasr, who provides us with invaluable insight into the general underlying challenges of the region. Additionally, there are unique and often proud differences in the identity of ethnic groups such as Egyptians, Turks, Arabs, and Persians, to name a few. Other areas in the Middle East are poly-cultural such as Afghanistan, North Africa, and Pakistan. Leadership requires situational awareness and understanding, which allows varied leadership to meet the demands generated by the circumstances (House, 2004).

Interpersonal mutual confidence, respect, and conviction is required before a working relationship of significance can be the basis for action and team-work. The Arab culture has a significant basis in personal relationship and trust and status. Greeting everyone based on status, starting with the leaders, elders, and seniors is important. Some common cultural courtesies are speaking only in response to direct questions and leaving specific discussion until after refreshments and small talk. Particularly, one should inquire about how life events are going for others. Mutual regard, common understanding, and common goals are required for a progressive working relationship. Attitudes set the tone for overcoming adversity and establishing a common vision and purposes. As situations change there is an expectation that the terms of an agreement or contract will be renegotiated to accommodate change and remain inclusive of common purpose. Attitude is an important issue to keep in mind as a leader. Leading means influencing, encouraging, nurturing relationships and making mutually beneficial advancements to a common objective; a positive, knowledgeable and respectful attitude will advance one's causes greatly and gain the admiration and respect of others.

Situational awareness and sensitivity with attention to interpersonal nuance and a higher level of patience are required in the Arab culture as opposed to western society. It is common in Arab culture to start a meeting with tea and discussions about one's health and family. If the principle is ready to discuss salient matters, he will bring up the topic for discussion when and if he feels it is appropriate. Some aspects of cognition, behavior, or affect may be particularly relevant in a specific country or region; evidence suggests that a core set of competencies enables adaptation to any culture (Hammer, 1987). This discussion reviews previous research on the variables of cross-cultural competence and intercultural effectiveness that contribute to desired outcomes.

The difference between western social norms of communication and interpersonal interaction in the Middle East is that communication is often not direct, but instead conveyed through body language and social actions. The timing of communication is essential due to cultural sensitivity. Group dynamics differ greatly from American preferences for the presentation of information and information exchange. There is a vast difference in the information that can be presented in a group as opposed to what can be discussed in private. T.E Lawrence noted the importance of using words sparingly in a group, but private opinions should be clearly and knowledgably voiced as well as clearly and diligently articulated. There is a greater sense of openness in a closed forum with a Middle East decision-maker (Lawrence, 2011b). Often, I would not participate in open forum discussion unless called upon to provide the position of those I represented or information that would clarify the discussion. My contribution was succinct and concise and I provided additional pertinent information upon request. The group looked to me as the source of information and understanding of outside positions and actions. I had become the honest broker. Infrequently, the group would ask what my thoughts were pertaining to a specific situation or individual; during such time times I used very few words, but conveyed the tone and accurate situational assessment even if it was not going to be well received.

If a Middle Eastern decision-maker fully buys into an idea, he takes ownership of the innovation. It is most important to support the idea agreed upon, as anything less would be a personal affront to the principle. As a personal and individual relationship is built, so was professional confidence and the ability to determine what could be accomplished and what could not be accomplished. One cannot expect to get all the concessions and achieve a mutual interest and participation in all actions. However, with the right leadership philosophies focused on the appropriate audience, a greater level of accomplishment is possible. It is better in a private setting to use candor and frank discussion while at the same time demonstrating intellectual command of the facts, perceptive flexibility, empathy, and solid situational awareness (Al-Omari, 2008). Leadership under difficult circumstances with a culture that is not similar to one's life experiences is an art of building a bridge to greater understanding, closer relations, and mutual trust and respect (Grisham, 2008).

Discussion

Cultural awareness is the study of cultural complexity and understanding. Ethical and effective leadership involves leading in a manner that respects the culture and dignity of others (Ciulla, 2014). As leaders are by nature in a position of social power, ethical leadership focuses on how leaders use ethical power in the decisions they make, actions they engage in, and ways they influence others (Gini, 1997). There are six key attributes that appear in ethical leadership: character and integrity, ethical awareness, community/people-orientation, motivating, encouraging and empowering, and managing ethical accountability (Resick, 2006). Middle Eastern priorities are contrasted much differently than other worldviews based on religious origins and may be in stark contrast to western ideals. The appropriate approach is based on understanding cultural perspectives and societal basis. Ethics and values are based on Islamic values and are deeply rooted in the cultural values of societies in the Middle Eastern culture just as Confucian values are pervasive throughout societies in the Confucian Asian cluster. When combined, these dimensions reflect leading in a manner that is respectful of the rights and dignity of others, which is, ethical leadership (Resick, 2006).

What separates a Middle Eastern culture into diverse segments and what binds the same culture together is a conglomeration of familial, tribal, religious, and regional norms. Considerate and diligent appreciative development of a situation determines the appropriate bridging strategies and advancement of relationships. Understanding the big picture, maintaining a positive attitude, and meaningful and purposeful communication often requires innovation and creative leadership (Tubbs, 2006). Situational awareness concerning culture is a driver for determining perspective, the origin of opinion, and belief. The deep meaningful development of how a high context culture is different and how to alter one's behavior and approach to it will greatly increase the level of success (Al-Omari, 2008).

What divides a culture is what matters in developing a relationship and appropriate cultural engagement. Cultural sub-division and belief can be the cause of great adamancy or radicalism for others to follow and demand submission. General culture is a fine starting point, but often we find adamant individuals in the subculture that are not present in the mainstream culture (Wardi, 2008). An example is a great divide between Kurdish culture and Shiite beliefs. While much animosity exists between the two entities, it was a puzzling observation that Shiite officials would make a deliberate effort to vacation in and even own houses in the Kurdish area of Iraq. At times, it seems that the animosity was predominantly verbal, yet, when the Kurds would try to further separate themselves from Iraq, it was met with visceral negative reaction. An interesting side note is that many that voiced a negative reaction to the Kurds also maintained vacation homes in the area because it was safer than other regions in Iraq. Understanding cultural nuances big and small as well as the level of conviction is sometimes one of the most important matters of innovation leadership in culture. It provides the basis of perspective, morals, and ethics of individuals and groups.

T.E. Lawrence gives us a historical basis for more current decision-making frameworks for this particular subculture. The leader's circumstances and situation dictated how he or she was to approach a situation within the cultural context. The context and principle of the 27 Articles remain valid today. The culture has remained similar and primarily intact over time (Lawrence, 2011b). Building alliances within the framework of existing culture is critical in influencing and leading. A leader is required to forge mutual relationships of trust and interest to influence those with a common interest. Working to develop a rapport to gain trust and acceptance in another culture that is at a different level of context and communication complexity is required to influence as well as to establish working relationships close enough to the primary leader to be addressed as an important member of the family, at times, even closer than some of the primary leader's own sons (Lawrence, 2011a).

Gaining the confidence of others, through innovation leadership and strong relationships generates a leadership role that is supported as part of a teamwork, but, in the Arab culture, is best done through good followership and support of the decision maker. Working with other cultures to gain trust, build respect, advance mutual projects and develop working relationships is supported by innovation leadership. The innovation is the bridging of cultures in such a manner as to demonstrate the credibility of a close advisor. The ability to frame actions in a mutually beneficial and culturally sensitive manner to gain the optimal potential allowed by the situation and circumstances is the goal (Kellerman, 1988).

Summary

This chapter offers a review of flexibility and adaptability when generating innovation in a multi-cultural context. Subtle divides can be considered unacceptable rifts when friction between contiguous cultures can heat up. It is important to know and understand the flashpoints in a poly-cultural environment. Again, situational awareness and cultural acceptance is paramount to developing influence. One need not take sides, but instead focus should be placed on the awareness that there are dissimilarities, what and where they are, and the ability to bridge the differences. The example used in this chapter is the various Muslim cultures found in the Middle East (Bueno, 2004).

The largest divide is between Sunni and Shiite theologies that manifest in the perspectives of the faithful. Each religious bifurcation has a certain view of themselves, the world, leadership, and social approach. As the world becomes more global, there are many fractures in society and social differences. These nuances both subtle and obvious generate a fluid matrix for innovation leadership based on situation and circumstance. Cultural situational awareness was the basis for influencing others, generating respect, and establishing mutual interests in dancing actions. The world may always have a division between and within societal elements, the extent of which can be bridged by innovation leadership. It is important to achieve awareness and understanding of these differing sentiments and use the difference to generate a positive perspective outcome for stakeholders through innovation and creativity. Exceptional communication and understanding based on positive attitude, leadership, a desire to lead change, and teamwork produces extraordinary results. One must remain flexible and agile in thought and action with sensitivity toward a host culture and its nuances. The ability to work between cultural divides is often determined by the ability a leader has to generate situational awareness and adapt to various situations and circumstances generated by this differentiation (Wunderle, 2006).

References

Al-Omari, J, 2008, *Understanding the Arab Culture: A Practical Cross-Cultural Guide to Working in the Arab World*, Hachette, New York.

Bates, DG and Rassam, A, 2001, *Peoples and Cultures of the Middle East*, Prentice Hall, Upper Saddle River, NJ.

Bueno, CM and Tubbs, SL, 2004, 'Identifying global leadership competencies: An exploratory study', *Journal of American Academy of Business*, vol. 5, no. 1, pp. 80–87.

Ciulla, JB, 2014, *Ethics, the Heart of Leadership*. ABC-CLIO, Santa Barbara, CA.

Elbadawi, I and Makdisi, S, 2010, *Democracy in the Arab World: Explaining the Deficit*. Routledge, London.

Gini, A, 1997, 'Moral leadership and business ethics', *Journal of Leadership & Organizational Studies*, vol. 4, no. 4, pp. 64–81.

Grisham, T and Walker, DH, 2008, 'Cross-cultural leadership', *International Journal of Managing Projects in Business*, vol. 1, no. 3, pp. 439–445.

Hammer, MR, 1987, 'Behavioral dimensions of intercultural effectiveness: A replication and extension', *International Journal of Intercultural Relations*, vol. 11, no. 1, pp. 65–88.

House, RJ, Hanges, PJ, Javidan, M, Dorfman, PW and Gupta, V, 2004, *Culture, Leadership, and Organizations: The Globe Study of 62 Societies*. Sage Publications, Thousand Oaks, CA.

Kellerman, B and Rubin, JZ, 1988, *Leadership and Negotiation in the Middle East*. Praeger Publishers, Santa Barbara, CA.

Lawrence, TE, 2011a, *Evolution of a Revolt*. Praetorian Press, Seattle, WA.

Lawrence, TE, 2011b, *Twenty-Seven Articles*. Praetorian Press, Seattle, WA.

Lawrence, TE and Calder, A, 1997, *Seven Pillars of Wisdom*. Wordsworth Editions, Ware, UK.

Nasr, V, 2007, *Shia Revival: How Conflicts within Islam Will Shape the Future*. W.W. Norton & Company, New York.

Polk, WR, 2006, *Understanding Iraq: A Whistlestop Tour from Ancient Babylon to Occupied Baghdad*. IB Tauris, New York.

Polk, WR, 2009, *Understanding Iran: Everything You Need to Know, from Persia to the Islamic Republic, from Cyrus to Ahmadinejad*. Palgrave Macmillan, New York.

Resick, CJ, Hanges, PJ, Dickson, MW and Mitchelson, JK, 2006, 'A cross-cultural examination of the endorsement of ethical leadership', *Journal of Business Ethics*, vol. 63, no. 4, pp. 345–359.

Tubbs, SL and Schulz, E, 2006, 'Exploring a taxonomy of global leadership competencies and meta-competencies', *Journal of American Academy of Business*, vol. 8, no. 2, pp. 29–34.

Wardi, A, 2008, *Understanding Iraq: Society, Culture, and Personality.* Edwin Mellen Press, Lewistown, NY.

Wunderle, WD, 2006, *Through the Lens of Cultural Awareness: A Primer for the United States Armed Forces Deploying in Arab and Middle Eastern Countries.* Government Printing Office, Washington DC.

12 Innovation on a small farm

Debra (Keppy) Arnoldsen and Mike Erdman

In 2011, Keppy and Ron Arnoldsen developed a vision for a small farm that wasted little, and typical plant and animal wastes produced value both for the farm and for others. Achieving this vision was a long and challenging road that required developing technologies and patents and a tremendous investment of effort on their part, as well as engaging the minds and energies of others. Many small farms create huge amounts of organic waste from their daily operations. Often, this is accumulated in large compost piles that are turned periodically and used on the farm. Sometimes these wastes are hauled away at a cost to landfills or by others to create mulch or compost. The Arnoldsens decided they could improve on these cumbersome or costly means of waste disposal and perhaps they could use the waste to create value on the farm. Their hopes were that they could eventually share this technology with other small farmers, who in turn could convert food and farm wastes into nutrients for their own use. Collectively, it might make a difference in the food waste cycle.

In this chapter, the reader will see how this need to utilize wastes and improve performance on their farm led to an innovation; the creation of a small-farm anaerobic digester and the generation of a new business and fertilizer product. By creating useful products from wastes, nutrients are sequestered to provide a fertilizer product useful for plant production technologies such as soil-less hydroponics and traditional gardening. The reader will see how this simple innovation started a quest for the Arnoldsens to improve the recycling of nutrients. Their journey is documented from idea formulation through prototype development to system refinements. The many challenges they faced and collaborations they formed along the way were important to their success. The reader will learn how they overcame these obstacles to continue inventing and improving the system used to accomplish their recycling goals. They will also learn why collaborations and partnerships are an integral component to their success. These are presented here to give the reader a better understanding of their journey and a clearer perspective of the value gained when you involve others and build a support system.

Description

The key to this innovation was the development of an anaerobic digester system that could be used to recycle farm manures and food wastes on small farms. Large farms currently use this technology but they typically install high-cost, large-scale digesters used to process vast quantities of farm wastes primarily from dairy cows and pigs. These wastes are temporarily stored in large lagoon pits or underground storage tanks. Many smaller farms cannot afford these systems and their manure quantities are not substantial enough to warrant this scale of anaerobic digester. Small farms make up a large portion of our food production industry.

In 2009, there were nearly two million small farms in the United States, roughly 90% of all farms in the country. Each year, farm animals in the U.S. produce over 335 million tons of manure. A lactating dairy cow can produce 150 pounds of manure every day, 20 broiler chickens produce over four pounds per day. Not only is this a challenge, but the potential for turning this waste into value is tremendous. Opportunity and need often combine to drive innovation.

The system of anaerobic digestion relies on bacterial decomposition in the absence of oxygen. The products that are generated in digester systems are called effluent, or sometimes digestate, containing both solid and liquid portions. A gas is generated called biogas that contains methane which is an important energy source. The Arnoldsens use it to heat pasteurize the liquid portion of the digester effluent that they use as the base for their fertilizer product, thus eliminating potentially harmful pathogens making the product safer for food production.

The story

Ron and Keppy Arnoldsen bought their 11-acre plot in Cornpropst Mills, Pennsylvania, in the late fall of 2006. Their dreams were to have a place where they could keep their horses, raise farm animals, and produce organic food. Years of hard work followed, spent installing utilities and driveways, building the barn and coops, drilling a well, and constructing high tunnel greenhouses and establishing garden beds. This labor of love was a challenge that enriched their lives and started them on their path of home food production and eventually a need to address the wastes generated. Their philosophy was to keep a small footprint on the land by recycling all of the wastes generated. On their farm, they wanted to build a device to utilize and incorporate all the resources provided by the many tenants and crops. When trying different existing approaches, they found areas for improvements especially for manure management. They wanted to create a system that was more efficient and easier to operate than compost piles or spreading of nutrients on their fields.

One day, Ron and Keppy were having a discussion over lunch about this need to repurpose wastes generated on the farm. Ron grabbed a napkin and sketched an idea he had for processing the farm wastes using a large underground section of pipe. They thought the idea would also be a benefit for odor abatement and began expanding on the engineering of such a device. After much research, discussion, and drawing, they finally agreed to pursue their innovation. The saga continued over a journey of six years and many modifications along the way. Eventually, they developed and patented their segmented anaerobic digester system, but not until it went through three major changes in the first two years of development. Some challenges left them wishing they had more engineering experience and they thought that input from other engineers might be wise. So, they looked at local programs and collaborative options for help. They also felt that surrounding themselves with others who had faith in their project, would give them motivational support.

The Arnoldsens applied to sponsor a Senior Capstone Project for Penn State's Engineering students in a program called the Learning Factory. They put together a basic poster of their ideas for the recruiting event where students from the various engineering departments could search for their senior capstone projects. Six students from biological, agricultural, and energy engineering colleges selected them as their sponsor. They spent the rest of the semester helping the Arnoldsens in several important ways. They created the CAD drawings to accompany their patent application that detailed the specifics of the digester body and segmented sections used to process inputs. They also helped design and re-design the separator plates, as well as a warming system for the underground pipe from solar thermal heat. The last two weeks of that semester, they helped install the first prototype and erect the greenhouse enclosure around it. This collaboration yielded much insight and support for the Arnoldsens enabling them to move forward with the construction phase. The fresh input of ideas and view of the different approaches was the motivation they needed.

Another collaboration was born that same semester when four Smeal Business College finance students used the Arnoldsens project to develop a business plan for a class requirement. They suggested marketing ideas and evaluated the potential budget and cash flow. Since the Arnoldsens needed additional funding to further their efforts, they accepted loans from six friends to help manage costs, eventually paying them back at a nice interest rate. The relationships that were forged with their investors and their moral support for the project continue today.

Over the next few years, several major modifications were made to the plate designs that separated the segments within the digester body. There were many smaller changes implemented, as well as unexpected needs. That winter, the solar panel feed lines froze during an electrical outage that disabled the circulating pumps despite the use of antifreeze solution. Gas collection was inefficient due to leaks in the system from where holes were cut in the pipe during the prototype development stage. They struggled with some of these challenges and decided to support yet another group of engineering students in the Learning Factory. Once again, they hoped that further intellectual support might bring ideas for some of the needed improvements and that the additional support would help them stay focused and motivated in their long struggle.

Since they were not completely satisfied with the functional attributes and mechanical movement of the separator plates, the Arnoldsens settled on installing large drums in each segment which was an idea supported by the students that semester. So, they tested it with small 50-gallon drums and designed a device to move the drums through the pipe when full and at a heavy weight load. That semester the students reconstructed the solar panel and built a bigger biogas collection bag. With their help and renewed motivation, the prototype was mostly completed. Testing and trials for waste inputs began on this smaller drum set up and the Arnoldsens installed full-size 110 gallon drums and improved the handling system once again. They were pleased with the products the system provided including the nutrient-rich liquid portion and the well decomposed solid "compost-like" portion.

Innovations are very valuable if there is an applied benefit to the market. The Arnoldsens realized that marketing and financial planning would be keys to their success and they knew that these were areas where they could improve their expertise. Keppy decided to pursue involvement with the Ben Franklin Technology program offered at the Penn State Research Park. It was a fairly new program developed for innovators with new potential inventions to help with development research and potential funding ideas. This eight week course was very beneficial in that it brought both marketing insight and inspired even more research to improve their knowledge in the field of digester businesses around the world. It was at this point in their journey that the Arnoldsens decided to focus on marketing of the fertilizer product, rather than the digester itself.

That summer they started yet another collaboration, this time with the nonprofit group Solar Cities who specialize in bringing the technology of anaerobic digestion to others around the world using available resources in developing regions to create home-made units for cooking fuel. It turned out a valuable relationship, where both the nonprofit and the Arnoldsens reaped benefits. In 2016, they agreed to install a second digester; a single batch-type unit they made of concrete. This was beneficial to the founders of Solar Cities who could use it as a display unit in central Pennsylvania where others could see the technology in use. This second digester turned out to be valuable for the Arnoldsens in its additional generation of methane and ability to process some more of their farm wastes. Now, leaky collection pipes did not plague the amount of gas yielded. A copious amount of biogas was created that could now be put to use for testing and refining their pasteurization ideas. Probably the most important benefit of all was that this sharing of knowledge and technology forged friendships and brought more insight for both. This area of technology is still in development worldwide. The Arnoldsens received a patent for their compartmentalized anaerobic digester and they still maintain the relationships they forged over the years. Today, this underground system provides a rich liquid, made from 100% recycled materials that is used as the base for their product, a liquid fertilizer amendment they now call Fertili-Tea.

Discussion

The concept that one can recycle nutrients bound up in food wastes by combining them with farm wastes and allowing the compound to decompose was not a new concept. However, the approach that the Arnoldsens used to accomplish this goal was new. It turned out to be a valuable innovation, despite requiring several changes to the prototype and many modifications of the device. Experimentation with inputs and their ratios and the effect on the products was also necessary over the years.

The Arnoldsens faced many challenges along the way, but they were determined to make it work. Their decision to incorporate inserted drums to both contain the valuable liquid product and improve the movement of the sections in their segmented design turned out to be a good switch. This change improved the process and made handling much more efficient. Though the whole journey and development was tiring, the necessary motivation came from their deep belief in the products created through this degradation process. The Arnoldsens shared a strong belief too that the input of others was important. Over the years, they continued with persistence and continued mechanical refinements. They knew that their perseverance could pay off in the long term and that, with patience, this system would yield many benefits. They refused to give up despite the long journey they were on. They realized that change was an integral part of the innovation process and that, with perseverance, these obstacles would be temporary. Over time, small changes in both the functional aspects of the device and the inputs of wastes and additives led to valuable improvements in their products and the nutritional aspects therein.

The Arnoldsens also felt strongly about self-education. They knew that they needed to continually improve their knowledge in this field and they educated themselves at each step along the way. Much research was acquired to stay abreast of the industry and new changes in this quickly developing field of anaerobic digestion. They learned what the best practices were and studied the designs of other systems in order to advance their own ideas and provide insight into areas where improvements could be made. The scrubbing of the biogas to remove sulfur was one such example and yielded a much safer fuel source.

Collaboration and networking were the key ingredients to their success. They reached out to others and found programs that might aid their efforts. This search incorporated many facets of innovation leadership from engineering and design to funding opportunities and marketing. Their journey was one that included a deep dedication to their innovation; one that they refused to give up on, despite the many challenges. Their own partnership was probably the most important reason for their success, as there exists a special way that Ron and Keppy complemented each other in both knowledge and abilities. Ron's mechanical knowledge and innate engineering capabilities provided the vital component needed to create, develop and advance the prototypes for the digester. Keppy's biology background, research abilities and business senses provided them with necessary motivation in these regards. When an innovation or improvement was needed, they did the needed research and then worked together to come up with a solution or a means to accomplish their goals. Overcoming hurdles became a necessary part of their innovation process.

There were other benefits as well in the learning experiences they provided to the two Penn State University senior capstone design engineering teams and several student interns over the years as well. They participated in two finance/marketing programs at Penn State that also provided opportunities and helped the Arnoldsens to foresee markets they could target and realize ways to finance the innovation. They also networked and consulted with an international program that brings this technology to impoverished areas to facilitate cooking and heating. In the future, they hope that these small-scale anaerobic digesters can be readily available to others so that the energy generated can bring about positive change in people's lives and this means of recycling can provide the necessary nutrients for healthy plant production.

Summary

Successful innovation requires that leaders be open to modifications and change. The Arnoldsens had to overcome many obstacles. Their investment of time and devotion to the innovation are demonstrated in the story of their six-year journey to having a marketable product. One major struggle was to keep forward momentum and make positive progress. Here are some of their final thoughts on ways to develop a successful innovation. Surround yourself with a positive support system and reach out to others. Having partners or colleagues that complement you can bring out alternative perspectives. The Arnoldsens surrounded themselves with support along the way and this was important in their success story. Remember that innovation requires much endurance and patience. The Arnoldsens are not alone in their long journey toward success. Many innovations require much time for development and this timeline can often become longer than expected. Be willing to educate yourself, be open to the ideas of others, and continue to further your expertise. Search out programs that can further your efforts from a business, engineering, or financial perspective. Believe in your idea, whether it is novel, needed, or just a better way of doing something. Try to stay positive no matter how long it takes. Positive motivation and attitudes can be contagious, inspire others to become involved, and be part of your support system. The results can be amazing!

References

Cornell University, 2017, 'Small farm statistics'. Available at http://smallfarms.cornell.edu/about/statistics-and-information-resources/ [Accessed 25 Aug. 2017].

Danovich, T, 2014, 'What to do with all the poo?' *Modern Farmer*. Available at: http://modernfarmer.com/2014/08/manure-usa/ [Accessed 25 Aug. 2017].

USDA, 2017, 'Farming and farm income'. *Economic Research Service*. Available at https://www.ers.usda.gov/data-products/ag-and-food-statistics-charting-the-essentials/farming-and-farm-income/ [Accessed 25 Aug. 2017].

13 Successful innovation in the public sector

Catherine Haynes

Innovation comes in many forms, in this chapter we will talk about a successful innovation within a government agency. It is about how I used my skills and experience as human resource manager to review procedures, train, and to prepare seven human resource assistants working in five states for a major organization inspection. Reading this chapter, you will learn that there are many ways to make innovation a success. Interactive training, consistency, and goal setting were key factors in this successful innovation. Over a one year period, it was my responsibility to ensure seven human resource offices would pass inspection based on predetermined guidelines. To accomplish this, I used face-to-face visits, conference calls, and inter-office courier mail to communicate with assistants. Your experience can be just the thing that an organization needs, share your knowledge.

Description

This is the overview of the organization's structure. Our unit in the organization consisted of approximately 800 employees. As the senior human resources manager, I had seven direct report human resource assistants in five eastern states. Each office served about 80–120 employees; they all have the same core responsibility of running the day-to-day office operations, conduct promotion proceedings, conduct required section training, and submit employee evaluations, submit award recommendations, and submit Equal Employment Opportunity (EEO) Reports. Their reports, proceedings and evaluations were submitted to corporate office either monthly or quarterly.

The inspections were conducted to measure the extent of uniformity throughout the organization by way of compliance with organizational rules and regulations. It was the commander's responsibility to ensure these actions were completed correctly and in a timely manner. The commander then distributed portions to the appropriate managers; for example, the human resources manager was responsible for all matters pertaining to personnel. Then, each person in the organization participated in the inspection based on their individual specialized job. Commanders receive a yearly evaluation report which reflects the result of the inspection.

The evaluation is a critical part of their consideration for promotion to the next level.

The story

The commander wanted a human resources manager who could bring all seven sites in his command under one standard operating procedure. Only one of his seven human resources sites received commendations and two received passing grades on the last inspection. He had four sites that needed to be in compliance with the rules and regulations and one year to get this done. Some of his observations were inconsistencies when each site completed reports, employee requests and employee personnel actions. Some were late while others were submitted with missing information. This had a negative impact on the employees and the human resources assistants. The HR assistants were not experienced enough and they needed someone at headquarters with more experience to evaluate and train them.

For the first month or so my boss and I went to the seven sites to meet with all the human resources assistants, section chiefs and first-line supervisors, although the main topic of discussion was the upcoming inspection from headquarters. I took notes as they expressed their concerns on matters related to human resources. This organization had to be ready for a week-long comprehensive inspection by a team of 10–15 subject matter experts. As I accompanied my boss, I learned much about the sites, the organization and its culture. I believe that culture at each site, even though it is part of the organization, reflects the style of its leader. My boss knew about my 17 years' experience in the organization as well as my work on the west coast inspection team as the subject matter expert on human resources. He wanted me to get the human resource sites of the organization ready for inspection the next year. Together we came up with a timeline and guidance.

Using the timeline and general guidance from my boss, I contacted each site human resource assistant. I met with each one individually in their office and treated them to lunch as an informal opportunity to get acquainted. I wanted them to know what strengths I brought to the organization, I talked about my prior assignments as the Employee Evaluation Team Leader, as the Equal Employment Opportunity Advisor, as the Senior Instructor for Unit Training and finally my last assignment as part of the west coast inspection team. I also needed them to understand how important the inspection was to the organization, our boss, and to them as the onsite human resource assistant. We all needed to be on the same page with procedures and reporting requirements per headquarters mandate so we could pass with the highest commendations. We had several rounds of meetings and then decided the best way to prepare for the inspection would be through a series of conference calls, site visits, and by updating the Standard Operating Procedures (SOP) Manual. We agreed that I would report our specific human resource progress to my boss then general overview to everyone else during headquarter's weekly meetings.

Weekly conference calls were the first part of the plan in preparation for the inspection. My goal was to use the final result report from the last inspection as a preparation guide for this inspection. I divided the results into sections so we could cover small portions during our conference calls and the whole would be completely reviewed about three months before the next inspection. I was the lead on the first few calls. But, I noticed that some assistants were not participating on calls and others were absent. So, I decided that each week someone else would take the lead on the calls. We would work on the agenda a few days before, and then the lead for that week would send it to everyone. We established guidelines for our calls so we could have a productive meeting. We all agreed that conference calls would be a very productive way to get prepared for the inspection. During one of our weekly conference calls, we had a stand in for an assistant who could not make the call. The representative had a list of questions about a procedure. He explained that he submitted an employee request several times and each time it was rejected. At this point he was getting ready to give up. He recognized he had been using the wrong procedure but did not know how to fix it. He wanted to know if the group could help. As a group, we answered all his questions. The assistant was present at the next conference call and reported that the guidance we gave his assistant was great. He was able to change the procedure for a successful result. The weekly conference calls progressed from questions about the written procedures for the inspection to conversations about making improvements in their area of responsibility that would go beyond the inspection. We completed the checklist for the inspection but there were more tasks in the organization to prepare for. The group felt that they had more to contribute. I presented a list of their ideas to my boss at our weekly meeting and he approved almost of them.

Site visits were another part of the plan to get ready for the inspection. My visit to the sites began about three weeks after our first conference call. I started with the site closest to the organization headquarters. My intent was to use this site as test model before going to the others which, because of their location, would be a three-day visit. After the visit to the first site, I made some changes to my procedures then coordinated my visits to the other sites. After visiting all the sites, the results were mixed, the three sites had very experienced human resource assistants. Two had intermediate experience and two had very little experience. My boss was concerned about the latter. I decided to use on-the-job training and peer to peer counseling between the individuals at the sites with the most experienced assistants and the sites with the least experienced. The sites with intermediate experience would be the back-up for the site with the most experience. They could also assist the rest of the team where needed.

A comprehensive written Standard Operating Procedures (SOP) Manual is the norm for a public organization; this SOP needed to be updated. Due to high turnover, it is widely considered the go-to publication for those who needed help completing specific tasks. It was normal for me to get a phone call from other managers in similar organizations asking for a copy of our operating procedures. Time is always of the essence, and written procedures, although time consuming for the initial preparation, are a piece of mind and ultimately time saving for subsequent users. Written procedures and examples result in uniformity; they establish consistency, and are in compliance with organization wide mandates. The sections of the SOP I updated based on my experience were discussed during our weekly conference calls. The goal was to have the manual completed and submitted for approval by the boss about two months prior to the company's inspection date.

About six months before the inspection the organization got copies of the current inspection checklist and a copy of the results of the last inspection. The results of our organization's last inspection were a consolidated report of about 150 pages that included all seven sites. I used the organization's copy of the last inspection to help create a timeline of completion for each section that would be inspected. Each site received copies of their individual site results and a copy of the current checklist. In our weekly conference calls, we discussed different sections of the checklist and how to improve them for the next inspection. During my monthly visits to the sites, I gave individual training to the assistants who needed it. Two months into the preparation, one of the three senior assistants was reassigned to a different organization. Her replacement arrived within one month. We did not adjust the schedule because she was familiar with the inspection protocol and was on board. We all recognizes the importance of this inspection so we worked hard using the tools of the past inspection and the checklist in order to pass it.

It took us nine months working as team to be ready for the inspection. We were able to present the boss with the standard operating procedures to review and sign one month ahead of schedule. The assistant at all seven sites then received their copies. The boss made extra copies and an electronic copy of the SOP. One month prior to the inspection we had our last conference call to cover the day of inspection procedures and to ask questions that might be asked. The assistants had copies of the inspection team schedule so they knew when the team would be at their site. I wanted to make sure they understood the significance of the inspection to them, the organization, and to the boss.

The inspection team arrived. That morning was electric. We had done all the preparation and our human resource office was ready. It was on organization wide inspection but we served as the administrative hub for the organization. We arranged the conference room to be the team's office/meeting place for the duration of the inspection. During the in-briefing my boss introduced her senior managers and in turn the leader of the team introduced the key team members. Since we had seven different sites the team comprised 20 inspectors instead of 15. The team leader explained the procedures and the agenda for the week. Then the inspection began. Some team members were accompanied by other members of the organization to the different sites. The hyper activates with the inspectors lasted four days. During that time if the team found a deficiency the section was given the opportunity to make corrections and to get re-inspected before the end of the 4th day. The morning of the out-briefing day was calm and quiet. We were about to find out if a year of preparation through hard work, dedication, and determination would pay. It did. As an organization, we passed with high recommendations; minor deficiencies were corrected before the end of the 4th day. The final report was signed by the team leader's boss and hard copies were to be sent to us. The team departed. The boss gathered all the managers and supervisors in the conference room to express his appreciation for a job well done. He recognized our hard work and team efforts to make this day a success.

Discussion

Carmeli (2010) theorized about the importance of innovation leadership in enhancing organization performance. I was the new leader in the organization tasked to provide guidance and improvement to merge the seven human resources sites into one cohesive unit. I met with the human resource assistants face to face. We were to share new ideas and methods that would improve performance on this next inspection but first we had to get to know each other. We met in their office and then, to keep the conversation going with a personal touch, I treated them to lunch. Later they were introduced to my predecessor via a conference call. I asked them what changes they wanted to see and what their most successful accomplishment was. This provided the opportunity for them to talk about themselves and for me to understand where they were with experience and training. This organization needed new ideas on how to assist the personnel at the sites.

Interactive training is one of the tools that allows more experienced employees to pass knowledge to other employees while keeping them engaged and more receptive to the new information (McMenimen, 2003). Our discussions were one of the ways for me to pass my skills and knowledge onto them. This training was a method to get each employee proficient in the required tasks thus standardizing the procedure. I shared my knowledge of administrative procedures and trained everyone on how to complete the tasks. The most complicated tasks were duplicated in the standard operating manual that we all created. In his book on hands-on training, Sisson (2010) wrote that this type of training is reasonable and inexpensive. He also went on to write that the type of training is based on the experience of the teacher, (p.5). Hands-on training was conducted during my visits to each site. The hands-on training gave them practical knowledge and confidence. One advantage of hands-on training is that it applies immediately to the assistants' jobs. At the end of the training each assistant had standard operating procedures complete with examples they could use at any time. They also had copies they could take when they left this assignment. Consistency in the practical application of selected tasks was also critical to the successful innovation. Frost (2014) wrote that an organized training and development program ensures that employees have a consistent experience and background knowledge.

Consistency is relevant for processing personnel actions and reports that are in compliance with the organization's policies and procedures. Human resources assistants must be aware of the expectations within the company for us to have the best chance to meet or exceed expectations in the inspection. Knowing what to expect during the inspection helps the assistants remain calm. In order for that to happen, preparation before the inspection was important.

Another aspect of the innovation was goal-setting. It was very important for us to set goals as a team. Hollenbeck and Williams (1987) examined the role of perceived goal importance, self-focus and actual past performance on the goal-setting process. We used the timeline, the directions from the boss and the results of the last inspection as a guide to set our team goals. We had one year before the inspection to set goals. The acronym SMART is an established tool used to plan and achieve goals. There are many explanations for the acronym SMART, the most common one is that goals should be Specific, Measurable, Achievable, Realistic, and Timely. Prather (2005) explains that this goal-setting process works well when the goal is to improve an existing system that is well established. This worked best for us because there was a system already in place but it needed new innovations. As part of our goal-setting we agreed on weekly conference calls where full participation on calls was critical. If the primary could not make it, then an alternative person would participate. The calls were productive in that weekly progress towards the inspection date was discussed and input towards completion of the standard operating procedures was provided.

Summary

This chapter is about using one's knowledge and leadership ability to influence a process. It demonstrates that knowledge is powerful when shared. By using my experience as a team member and as a manager I was able to work with human resource associates located in five different states to successfully prepare for a major inspection from headquarters. I also recognize the importance of the teamwork; the assistants worked as hard as I did to achieve the goals we set. Throughout the entire process communicating with other team members was essential. We all understood that small steps, such as the conference calls and peer to peer counseling, were required to meet the ultimate goal of the successful inspection. As a result, the organization has an up-to-date standard operating procedure manual and all the human resources associates were trained. The process took nine months, several trips to five different states and several conference calls. At the end, we passed the inspection with high recommendations and many accolades.

It is important to recognize the self and the contributions you can make to the organization. My boss' confidence in my ability to lead the human resources office through the inspection was powerful. The associates relied on my experience as the subject matter expert to guide them through the process. Still, I did not do all the work, when we meet as a team each person left the meeting with a clear understand of what they had to do and what their deadline was. It was not always smooth, sometimes I would get a phone call that someone could not attend and there was no replacement. In that case, one of us who are not leading the call will take notes and call the absent member to share the proceedings. Employees don't like change; they want to keep doing procedures and steps the same way because they know it. Learning some new procedure can be frustrating, fearful, and time consuming. Supervisors should assist in the training of the workers. Successful training does not have to be formal but it should be interactive and relevant.

References

Carmeli, A, Gelbard, R and Gefen, D, 2010. 'The importance of innovation leadership in cultivating strategic fit and enhancing firm performance', *The Leadership Quarterly*, vol. 21, no. 3, pp. 339–349.

Frost, S, 2014, 'The importance of training & development in the workplace', *Chron.* Available at http://smallbusiness.chron.com/importance-training-development-workplace-10321.html [Accessed 25 Aug. 2017].

Hollenbeck, JR and Williams, CR, 1987, 'Goal importance, self-focus, and the goal-setting process', *Journal of Applied Psychology*, vol. 72, no. 2, p. 204.

McMenimen, K and Sack, MP and Rume Interactive, 2003. *Interactive Training Method for Demonstrating and Teaching Occupational Skills*. U.S. Patent 6,514,079.

Prather, CW, 2005, 'The dumb thing about SMART goals for innovation', *Research Technology Management*, vol. 48, no. 5, p. 14.

Sisson, K, 2010, 'Employee relations matters', *Cornell University ILR School*. Available at http://digitalcommons.ilr.cornell.edu/reports/29/ [Accessed 25 Aug. 2017].

14 Innovation leaders in healthcare

Maureen Connelly Jones

Innovations occur every day in the healthcare industry in the form of new medications, new treatments, and novel implementations of prior treatments. Effective healthcare leaders are leading innovation regularly. This chapter will explore two innovation leaders in healthcare and how their actions benefited their employees, organizations, and patients. The story will also examine how these Chief Executive Officers (CEOs) worked to create a culture of continuous innovation. The chapter will focus on their influence on the people around them and discuss previous research on the characteristics that made them successful innovation leaders.

Description

Matt and Kate are CEOs who lead healthcare organizations and who are both successful because of their leadership style. Vice presidents in their organizations have seen the positive impact of Matt's and Kate's actions in themselves and others (Jones, 2014). They demonstrate a strong level of engagement, trust, and support. When leading innovation, creative work often springs from the choices made by CEOs. The leadership characteristics demonstrated by Matt and Kate embrace the competency model of innovation leaders (Gliddon, 2006). Each leader takes action to support idea generation within their executive leadership group, identifies innovations, and encourages others to do the same.

Because of their inclusive, supportive, and empowering leadership styles, they have worked with their team to evaluate and implement innovations brought forth by a diverse array of team members at many different levels in their organizations. Their executive team has a high level of engagement and openness. By building a culture of continuous innovation, this positive attitude circles back up with a multitude of organizational benefits including idea-sharing, ethical patient-focused decision-making, and advocacy for others. They also embrace both exploratory and value-added innovations. The healthcare industry is an important place to grow both types of innovations. New ideas need to be considered as well as modifying existing ideas in order to continue to evolve better patient care and improved outcomes.

In a hospital, outpatient clinic, or long-term care facility, employees may be asked to adopt a policy, procedure or process as the result of regulatory changes, insurance payment adjustments, special emergencies, or new research. There is a fatigue that accompanies this type of change, but innovation leaders find a way to open channels of communication, rally their employee base, and focus on why the change needs to happen. For example, when a CEO uses their high level adaptive abilities coupled with an aptitude for leveraging resources, they can help executive leadership team members and employees decrease the change fatigue by scanning for organizational needs that, in turn, prepare employees to react in unison rather than in reactive crisis mode (Jones, 2014).

Innovation leaders in healthcare focus on building organizational talent to assure that, whenever a challenge presents itself, they are able to view it from multiple perspectives which can often lead to innovation. When a CEO shares the same perspectives with executive or mid-level leadership teams, they then empower those they lead. The focus of this chapter is to demonstrate how the interactions between the CEOs and their leadership teams forged a culture of continuous innovation within their organizations. When a CEO actively engages their direct reports and other employees, the interactions breed innovation as a result of role modeling and support. Likewise, these interactions can form an innovation network team that helps to solve problems at different levels in the organization. Although these two stories are set in healthcare, the characteristics and actions explored may be applicable to innovation leaders in many other types of organizations.

The story

Matt's and Kate's stories will provide a fresh perspective on ways to understand innovation leadership in a healthcare environment. Healthcare has some unique needs when it comes to leadership and that opens up opportunities for those who can adapt quickly, leverage internal and external resources, create strategies to benefit the organization, utilize ethical decision-making, and continually build internal talent. Herzlinger (2006) suggests that the multitude of issues facing healthcare, such as medical errors, soaring costs, and the evolving landscape of regulatory changes, makes innovation difficult. Why is innovation trickier in healthcare versus say a technology company? When working with people, one cannot just create a prototype and keep trying until it works. As healthcare is focused on working with people, people's lives and well-being are at stake. For example, if a new cell phone application is developed and tested over and over again to see what works and what does not work, chances are no one may get hurt. That model is not as easily implemented within a healthcare environment. While innovations in patient treatments may be addressed in clinical studies, innovation with people is still well within the reach and responsibility of healthcare providers. The time spent fostering relationships within a healthcare organization can cultivate an exciting foundation for innovative thought and problem solving, a much-needed focus.

Change is no longer something sudden and sporadic. Instead it is a consistent force in the healthcare industry and something successful leaders engage in rather than run from. Many industries face regulatory changes and shifting market targets. This is also true for hospitals, long term care facilities, and physician practices, to name just a few. Healthcare leaders often need to shift an entire organization in order to respond to a new practice or reimbursement model. In doing so, they and their leadership team are charged with convincing the stakeholders of that organization to move along with them. These situations require that healthcare CEOs arrive with a skill-set ready to facilitate, identify and grow talent, have a vision beyond the current issues, and foster employee engagement that seeks pioneering solutions. Essentially, the leader needs to fit the organization and thus, the term executive fit applies to change. In a study by Chen (2012), it seems that fit is an evolving metric. Even though a leader might have been the best match at first, it does not necessarily mean they will continue to be so going forward. Executive leadership fit is a critical concept for healthcare CEOs because, without it, the daunting task of developing innovations for better healthcare outcomes may fall short for patients and for employees.

Our first innovation leader, Matt, is described by his subordinates as someone who allows them the freedom to look for new ideas and explore new solutions to the increasing challenges they face. He leads a team of executives at a medium sized acute-care facility. Matt helped to select the majority of the C-level leaders and says that he selected individuals who share his passion for excellence and inclusiveness. He also describes the importance of having each of his leadership team members share his vision for empowering employees to think outside the box. He believes that without this and a shared vision, it would be difficult to make many of the changes and adjustments that are a daily necessity of modern healthcare organizations (Jones, 2014).

When he took on the role of CEO, the organization was on the verge of bankruptcy. He knew what steps would need to be taken in order to turn the organization around and make it a competitor. This was no small task as this market was saturated with acute-care facilities vying for local patients. He took a slow and methodical approach addressing each aspect of the organization to build a shared mission and vision. During this transition, he utilized his skills to consider the financial needs of the organization and his employees (Jones, 2014).

Change was needed and innovations were a must. He set out to learn what each employee needed from him and how he would support their development. He understood that social infrastructure, in leadership, is where it all starts. He knew that if he developed the team and provided examples that set a strong precedent for role-modeling behaviors, each of his executive leaders would pass this knowledge along to their department directors and supervisors.

Matt was interested in the personal development of his employees. His level of engagement and concern included knowing the names of his employee's children and recent life events. This created a sense of loyalty toward the organization and was substantiated each time he visited employees. His executive leaders stated that he made a sincere connection, bringing about a true sense of caring and trust in their problem-solving abilities. His employees extended this approach to those around them, developing a willingness to think more broadly and deeply about solutions. But, how does this process start? Matt puts each person in the right place with the right assignment. His employees are free to share innovations and Matt provides validation by explaining how the innovations are making a difference. Understanding that a vice president may not get it right the first time and then mentoring them is critical (Jones, 2014). Matt makes sure each member of the team knows he has their back.

When his subordinates were asked about how he responded to daily crises, they described similar experiences of thinking beyond the current situation, networking, and making things happen. For example, Matt was able to use his networking abilities to find housing for a group of employees who had lost their homes. It was not typical of a CEO, but it met his employee's needs. That is innovation in this group of employees. He looked at a problem from different perspectives and it rubbed off on those around him. Matt was able to dive deep into details and develop broad strategy. In one instance, when the organization was struggling with a large-scale problem for which Matt was not an expert, he brought his team together, reminded them that they had the skills necessary to respond to the issue, and then let them lead. Three of his executive leaders were interviewed and all agreed that having his support allowed them perform their jobs with the confidence they needed to look for innovative solutions and to empower others to do the same (Jones, 2014). This is truly a gift in leadership and mentoring supports the development of innovations.

Our second innovation leader, Kate, has leadership characteristics that are similar to Matt's. She also carefully chose leaders who embodied her passion for thinking beyond and looking for new ways to develop solutions. Because she did not see her job as authoritative, she welcomed ideas and solutions that originated outside her office. She encouraged those working with her to think about how to motivate their employees to look beyond the expected. She stressed the importance of mentoring and that employee growth makes the organization grow (Jones, 2014). How was Kate different from the other leaders that her employees had worked for over the years? Her employees stated how personal her approach was, how she kept everyone in the loop, and how she brought her team closer by empowering them. She is a CEO who is part of her team and she encourages her team to be a part of her decisions to gain their buy-in. She encourages members of her team to be comfortable when coming to her with new ideas (Jones, 2014). Thus, innovation may more freely take place in environments where employees feel comfortable sharing new ideas and making decisions because their leader has made it clear that it is a safe place.

Kate believes in developing a process early and validating its importance with a variety of metrics. In regard to decision making, she stresses the importance of clear expectations, being decisive in crisis situations, and following through in the patient's best interest (Jones, 2014). Being inclusive is a powerful way to lead innovation and one has to consider many variables when caring for a patient. Although measuring innovation can at times be difficult, it is easy to see when a leader's actions create an environment of creativity and originality. The organizational culture shows little sign of stagnation. Innovation leaders and employees actively seek feedback, validation, and provide support to one another. One person can make a difference, and for the employees at these two healthcare facilities, a big difference was felt throughout the organization.

Discussion

CEOs who successfully lead healthcare organizations through a crisis were found to have similar characteristics. Eight themes emerged that suggested their success was rooted in their leadership behaviors, however, the biggest impact was the effect that the leader's behaviors had on others (Jones, 2014). These eight themes include: (a) letting leaders lead, (b) leveraging resources, (c) doing what is right, (d) crisis adaptability, (e) partnering, (f) building organizational talent, (g) meaningful visibility, and (h) strategic foresight. These themes, in combination with the competency model of innovation leaders, can build a foundation for developing innovation leaders in healthcare.

Madjar (2005) suggests that if an organization places a CEO who supports innovation at the helm, supports them emotionally, and provides them with adequate resources, the organization becomes innovative as the result of having that specific CEO at the helm. Dryer (2009) describes innovation as the secret sauce everyone was looking for in a leader and that top executives did not necessarily need to take on the burden of developing innovations, but instead facilitated others in doing so. The two leaders discussed in this chapter are examples of these concepts. Both Matt and Kate brought in employees they felt embodied their key characteristics. This is a critical step when a building a team that can think on their feet and make a difference throughout the organization (Jones, 2014). Dryer (2009) found that the most creative executives did five things well: (a) associating, (b) questioning, (c) observing, (d) experimenting, and (e) networking. Likewise, Dryer (2009) found that creative executives spent more than 50% of their time on these activities.

House's (1996) path-goal theory suggests that leaders make an impact when they directly connect with other employees (Jermier, 1996). Individual connections allow innovation leaders to know their followers. Understanding an employee's aspirations and skill set can lead to a mentoring experience that cultivates innovation. These leaders engage so often and with such a variety that followers feel empowered and trust that the CEO will consider their ideas. Likewise, they encourage a culture of continuous innovation throughout the organization. Matt and Kate displayed the characteristics of successful innovation leaders. Therefore, as we search for innovation leaders to solve the challenges facing the U.S. healthcare system, we may want to look for leaders who have many of the characteristics described in this chapter and throughout this book. Innovation leaders who are CEOs should be ready to lead at every level of the organization and personally mentor those they that they interact with most, their executive leaders.

Summary

The focus on innovation leadership in healthcare is due to the significant competition and economic uncertainties. Innovation leaders may give organizations an edge in a crowded marketplace. In an industry that must make safety and efficacy its top priority, there is a need to shift to a cutting-edge business mindset. The two leaders described in this chapter displayed the skills necessary to help those around them flourish. They helped to develop innovations that benefit patients and families who come to healthcare providers at the most vulnerable of times.

References

Chen, G and Hambrick, DC, 2012, 'CEO replacement in turnaround situations: executive (mis)fit and its performance implications', *Organization Science*, vol. 23, no. 1, pp. 225–243.

Dryer, JH, Gregersen, H and Christensen, CM, 2009, 'The innovators DNA', *Harvard Business Review*, Available at https://hbr.org/2009/12/the-innovators-dna [Accessed 25 Aug. 2017].

Gliddon, DG, 2006, 'Forecasting a competency model for innovation leaders using a modified Delphi technique'. PhD. The Pennsylvania State University.

Herzlinger, RE, 2006, *Who Killed Health Care?*McGraw-Hill Education, New York.

House, RJ, 1996, 'Path-goal theory of leadership: Lessons, legacy, and a reformulated theory', *Leadership Quarterly*, vol. 7, no 3, pp. 323–352.

Jermier, JM, 1996, 'The path-goal theory of leadership: A subtextual analysis', *Leadership Quarterly*, vol. 7, no 3, pp. 311–316.

Jones, MC, 2014, 'Leadership illuminated by crisis: Characteristics of effective hospital CEOs'. PhD. The Pennsylvania State University.

Madjar, N, 2005, 'The contributions of different groups of individuals to employees' creativity'. Available at https://pdfs.semanticscholar.org/def8/5f3bce1ce2c8b88ef42c19531dba9b630666.pdf [Accessed 25 Aug. 2017].

15 Afterword

David G. Gliddon

Welcome back explorers! What an amazing journey! We hope we inspired you to become an innovation leader. In closing, I'd like to reflect on a few more interesting innovations. In my classes, I often ask a reflective question. What's the oldest company in the world? Often, I get answers such as IBM, Ford, or GE. Although they are considered successful established companies in modern times, some of the oldest companies still in existence are actually over 1,000 years old. In fact, we probably don't really know what the oldest company in the world really is because trade is historically such an important human innovation.

I also like to ask another reflective question. What do you think are the society's most important innovations? There's no right answer of course, but I like to point out a few, like Gutenberg's printing press that revolutionized human learning. Another is electronic communication. From the advent of wired telegraphs, communicating over a distance has had a strong impact on society. With the development of Guglielmo Marconi's radio telegraphy, it became possible to wirelessly communicate. Today, this innovation is foundational in society and, in itself, is a critical part of how we create and diffuse other innovations.

When we think back on how many different innovations our lives are built upon, it highlights how many different innovation leaders it took to help create and diffuse those innovations. As an innovation leader, you may work on innovations that have a profound impact or those that just may help make daily life a happier place. But, innovations contribute to progress in society. I encourage you to read beyond this book about the innovation leaders that most interest you and the innovations that they created.

Index

Printed in the United States
by Baker & Taylor Publisher Services